HATCHMENTS IN BRITAIN

6

Cambridgeshire, Essex, Hertfordshire, Huntingdonshire and Middlesex

6

Cambridgeshire, Essex, Hertfordshire Huntingdonshire and Middlesex

Edited by

PETER SUMMERS, F.S.A.

and John Titterton

PHILLIMORE

1985

Published by
PHILLIMORE & CO. LTD.
London and Chichester

Head Office: Shopwyke Hall,
Chichester, Sussex, England

© Cambridgeshire — William A. Sanders
Essex — Christopher Harrold
Hertfordshire — A. W. Longden
Huntingdonshire — David C. Lane
Middlesex — J. D. Lee
1985

ISBN 0 85033 536 1

Typeset in the United Kingdom by:
Fidelity Processes - Selsey - Sussex

Printed and bound in Great Britain by
OXFORD UNIVERSITY PRESS

CONTENTS

ILLUSTRATIONS

GENERAL INTRODUCTION

Hatchments are a familiar sight to all those who visit our parish churches. They are not only decorative, but of great interest to the herald, genealogist and local historian. It is therefore surprising that — apart from local surveys in a few counties mostly in recent years — no attempt has yet been made to record them on a national scale. This series will, it is hoped, remedy the deficiency; it is proposed to publish separate volumes covering all English counties as well as Wales, Scotland and Ireland.

It is probable that no volume will be complete. Previously unrecorded hatchments will turn up from time to time; many have already been found in obscure places such as locked cupboards and ringing chambers. There are likely to be some inaccuracies, for hatchments are often hung high up in dark corners, and the colours may have faded or be darkened with age and grime. Identification is a problem if the arms do not appear anywhere in print: and even if the arms are identified, pedigrees of the family may not always be available. But enough has been done to make publication worth while; the margin to the pages will perhaps allow for pencilled amendments and notes.

Since I began the survey in 1952 many hatchments, probably evicted at the time of Victorian restorations, have been replaced in the churches when they came. On the other hand, during the same period just as many hatchments have been destroyed. An excuse often made by incumbents is that they are too far gone to repair, or that the cost of restoration is too great. Neither reason is valid. If any incumbent, or anyone who has the responsibility for the care of hatchments which need attention, will write to me, I shall be happy to tell him how the hatchments may be simply and satisfactorily restored at a minimal cost. It is hoped that the publication of this survey will help to draw attention to the importance of these heraldic records.

The diamond-shaped hatchment, which originated in the Low Countries, is a debased form of the medieval achievement – the shield, helm, and other accoutrements carried at the funeral of a noble or knight. In this country it was customary for the hatchment to be hung outside the house during the period of mourning, and thereafter be placed in the church. This practice, begun in the early 17th century, is by no means entirely obsolete, for about 80 examples have so far been recorded for the present century.

Closely allied to the diamond hatchment, and contemporary with the earlier examples, are rectangular wooden panels bearing coats of arms. As some of these bear no inscriptions and a black/white or white/black background, and as some otherwise typical hatchments bear anything from initials and a date to a long inscription beginning 'Near here lies buried . . .', it will be appreciated that it is not always easy to draw a firm line between the true hatchment and the memorial panel. Any transitional types will therefore also be listed, but armorial boards which are clearly intended as simple memorials will receive only a brief note.

With hatchments the background is of unique significance, making it possible to tell at a glance whether it is for a bachelor or spinster, husband or wife, widower or widow. These different forms all appear on the plate immediately following this introduction.

Royal Arms can easily be mistaken for hatchments, especially in the West Country where they are frequently of diamond shape and with a black background. But such examples often bear a date, which proves that they were not intended as hatchments. Royal hatchments, however, do exist, and any examples known will be included.

All hatchments are in the parish church unless otherwise stated, but by no means are they all in churches; many are in secular buildings and these, if they have no links with the parish in which they are now found, are listed at the end of the text. All hatchments recorded since the survey began are listed, including those which are now missing.

As with the previous volumes much work has been done in the past by many friends; their records have proved invaluable and greatly lessened the amount of research needed. As for those now responsible for each county who have checked and added to all these early records, I am most grateful for their care and efficiency. For this volume I have been much helped by John Titterton, who is now Assistant Editor, but who will be co-Editor for the remaining volumes of the series.

The illustrations on the following two pages are the work of the late Mr. G. A. Harrison and will provide a valuable 'key' for those unfamiliar with the complexity of hatchment backgrounds.

One last, but important note. Every copy sold of this book helps a child in the Third World; for I have irrevocably assigned all royalties on the entire series to a Charity, The Ockenden Venture.

PETER SUMMERS
Day's Cottage, North Stoke, Oxford

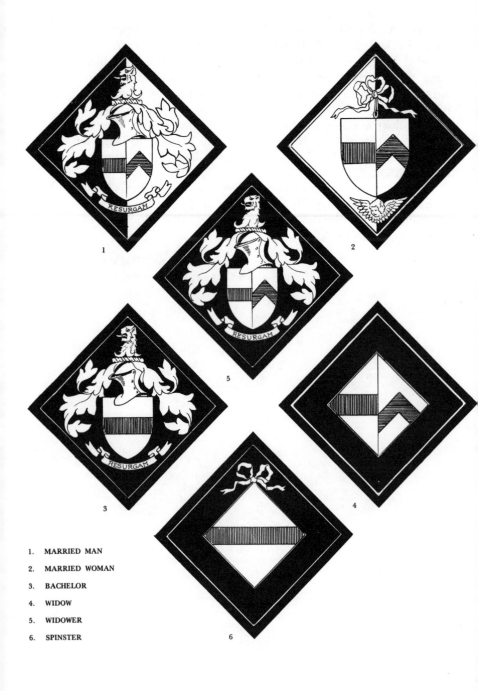

1. MARRIED MAN
2. MARRIED WOMAN
3. BACHELOR
4. WIDOW
5. WIDOWER
6. SPINSTER

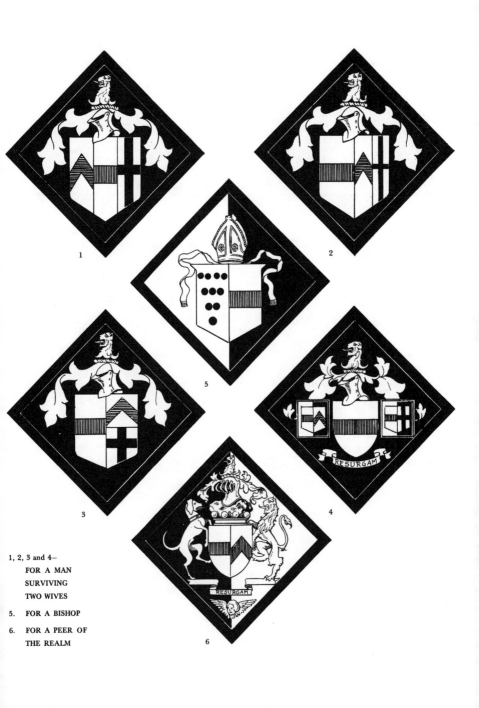

1, 2, 3 and 4—
FOR A MAN
SURVIVING
TWO WIVES

5. FOR A BISHOP

6. FOR A PEER OF
THE REALM

ABBREVIATIONS

B.P.	=	Burke's *Peerage, Baronetage and Knightage*
B.L.G.	=	Burke's *Landed Gentry*
B.E.P.	=	Burke's *Extinct and Dormant Peerages*
B.E.B.	=	Burke's *Extinct and Dormant Baronetcies*
V.C.H.	=	*Victoria County History*
D.N.B.	=	*Dictionary of National Biography*
M.I.	=	Monumental Inscription
P.R.	=	Parish Register
M.O.	=	*Musgrave's Obituary*
G.M.	=	*Gentleman's Magazine*
Gen. Mag.	=	*Genealogists' Magazine*
M.G. & H.	=	*Miscellanea Genealogica et Heraldica*
E.A.	=	*Elliott Armorial*
E.R.O.	=	*Essex Record Office*
Bloom	=	*Monumental Inscriptions, E.R.O.*
Cass	=	*History of East Barnet*
Cussans	=	*History of Hertfordshire*
Morant	=	*History of Essex*

NOTE

Blazons throughout are exactly as noted at the time of recording, not as they ought to be.

CAMBRIDGESHIRE

by

William A. Sanders

Babraham 1: For Jane Law, 1826
(Photograph by Mr. John Reiman)

INTRODUCTION

Most of the hatchments in the Cambridge area were first recorded for this survey by undergraduates in the mid-fifties and it is good to say that only two or three of these are no longer in their original positions. In several cases, notably at Babraham, Chippenham and Kirtling, the hatchments have been beautifully restored and rehung; and at Hinxton two have already been restored, the other five meanwhile having been carefully placed in a vestry.

There are at least six hatchments of the 17th century in the county, at Chatteris, Fordham and Sawston Hall, the latter being for Henry Hodelston who died in 1657; the Dayrell one at Fordham has not been fully identified, but it is very small and unusual in that it bears two shields and two small lozenges, all with impalements, as well as the main shield.

There are two 20th century hatchments at Swaffham Prior, although one of these is not properly a hatchment as it was erected by a widower, some years after the death of his wife, as a memorial. The most interesting modern example is probably that for A. C. Benson, which hangs in the ante-chapel at Magdalene College, together with the hatchment of S. A. Donaldson, his immediate predecessor as Master.

Among the Adeane hatchments at Babraham is an unusual one for Jane (Adeane), wife of the Rt. Rev. George Law, Bishop of Bath and Wells; this bears two shields, one with the arms of the See impaling Law, and the other with Law impaling Adeane. The marshalling of the arms on the hatchment of Henrietta Jeaffreson at Dullingham is even more unusual; the two lozenges are not accollé in the normal manner, but placed one above the other.

Although these volumes cover hatchments only I think I should make brief reference to the 17th century armorial board at St Michael's, Cambridge, the beautifully carved achievement of Henry Liyell at Bourn, and the two uninscribed

3

rectangular panels, now in the Wisbech Museum, to Bowyer Edward Sparke, Bishop of Ely, and his wife Hester, who died within days of each other in 1836.

I should like to thank my friend, Bill Roberts, who although living over the county boundary, at Great Chesterford, kindly assisted with checking hatchments in South Cambridgeshire. I must also thank Mrs. Rosemary Pardoe and Mr. S. A. Payne, who covered the northern parts of the county and the Isle of Ely.

William A. Sanders
Nine Chimney House, Balsham

Addendum

QUY

1. All black background
Or three pallets azure, on a chief gules three martlets or, in fess point a martlet sable for difference (Martin)
Crest: A marten-cat passant proper   Mantling: Gules and argent
Motto: In coelo quies
Probably for James Martin, Banker, M.P. for Cambridge, Lord of the Manor of Quy, who d. 15 Dec. 1744, aged 31.   (M.I.)

2. Sinister background black
Qly, 1st and 4th, Ermine two boars passant in pale gules, in centre chief the Badge of Ulster (Whichcote), 2nd and 3rd, qly i. & iv. Gules three ?cranes or (   ), ii. & iii. Gules a chief indented or (   )   In pretence, and impaling, Per saltire sable and or a lion rampant counterchanged (Gould)
For Jane, dau. and co-heiress of Sir Nicholas Gould, 1st Bt., who m. 1677, Sir Paul Whichcote, 2nd Bt., of Quy Hall, and d. 1698.   (B.P. 1905 ed.)

ABINGTON PIGOTTS

1. All black background
Qly, 1st and 4th, Sable three pickaxes within a bordure argent, a canton argent (Pigott), 2nd and 3rd, Argent a chevron between three buglehorns stringed sable (Foster)   In pretence: Qly, 1st and 4th, Sable three pickaxes within a bordure argent (Pigott), 2nd and 3rd, Azure three escallops in pale argent (Symes)
Crests: Dexter, A greyhound passant sable   Sinister, A stag's head erased sable attired or   Mantling: Gules and argent
Motto: Hoc age
For the Rev. William Foster Pigott, D.D., who m. 1788, Mary, only dau. of Grenado Pigott, of Ashton, Herefordshire, took the additional name of Pigott 1805, and d. 5 Feb. 1827. (Eton College Register 1753-1790)

2. All black background
On a lozenge   Qly, 1st and 4th, Sable three pickaxes within a bordure argent, a canton azure (Pigott), 2nd, Per pale argent and sable on a chevron per pale sable and or between three buglehorns stringed counterchanged two escallops counterchanged (Foster), 3rd, Argent a human heart gules imperially crowned or, on a chief sable three escallops or (Graham)   In pretence: Qly, 1st and 4th, Foster as 2nd, but no escallops, 2nd and 3rd, Argent on a bend azure between two cinquefoils sable three garbs or (   )
For Mary, only dau. and heir of the Rev. John Foster, D.D., Provost of Eton, who m. 1794, George Edward Graham-Foster-Pigott, of Abington Pigotts, and d. 25 Nov. 1858. He d. 5 Nov. 1832. (B.L.G. 1937 ed.)

BABRAHAM

1. Sinister background black
Two oval shields   Dexter, surmounted by a bishop's mitre, and with a crosier and key in saltire behind shield, Azure a saltire per saltire qly quartered or and argent (See of Bath and Wells), impaling, Ermine on a bend engrailed between two cocks gules three molets or (Law)
Sinister, surmounted by a cherub's head, Law, impaling, Sable on a chevron or between three griffins' heads erased argent three molets gules (Adeane)

5

For Jane, eldest dau. of General James Whorwood Adeane, who m.
1784, the Rt. Rev. George Henry Law, D.D., Bishop of Bath and
Wells, and d. 27 Sept. 1826. He d. 22 Sept. 1845.   (B.L.G. 1947
ed.; B.P. 1949 ed.; D.N.B.)

2. All black background
Qly of six, 1st and 6th, Adeane, as 1, 2nd, Argent a chevron between
three stags' heads cabossed sable (Whorwood), 3rd, Argent on a cross
sable a leopard's face or (Bridges), 4th, Argent a fess between three
martlets sable (   ), 5th, Or a pile gules (Chandos), impaling,
Argent a fret gules•(Blake)
Crest: A demi-griffin sable wings elevated argent collared or
Mantling: Gules and argent   Motto: Resurgam
For Robert Jones Adeane, who m. 1785, Annabella, dau. of Sir
Patrick Blake, 1st Bt., and d. 10 Jan. 1823.   (B.L.G. 1937 ed.;
M.I.)

3. Sinister background black
Qly, 1st, Sable on a chevron between three griffins' heads erased or
three molets sable (Adeane), 2nd, Argent a chevron sable between
three stags' heads cabossed gules (Whorwood), 3rd Bridges, 4th,
Chandos, impaling, Sable a lion rampant between three crosses formy
fitchy at the foot argent (King)   No motto   Shield surmounted
by two cherubs' heads
For Catherine Judith, dau. of John King of Aldenham House, Herts,
who m. 1822, as his 1st wife, Henry John Adeane, M.P. for
Cambridgeshire, 1830-32, and d. 27 June 1825.   (B.L.G. 1937 ed.;
M.I.)

4. Dexter background black
Qly, 1st, Adeane, as 3, 2nd, Whorwood, as 2, 3rd, Bridges, 4th,
Chandos, impaling, Argent on a bend azure three stags' heads cabossed
or (Stanley)
Crest: A demi-griffin wings elevated or collared sable   Mantling:
Gules and argent   Motto: Resurgam
For Henry John Adeane, M.P., who m. 2nd, Matilda Abigail, dau. of
John Thomas, 1st Baron Stanley of Alderley, and d. 11 May 1847.
(B.L.G. 1937 ed.)

5. All black background
On a lozenge surmounted by a cherub's head   Qly, 1st, Sable on
a chevron argent between three griffins' heads erased vert three
bezants (Adeane), 2nd, Argent a chevron sable between three stags'
heads cabossed proper (Whorwood), 3rd, Argent on a cross sable a
heart vert (Bridges), 4th, Chandos, impaling, Stanley   Skull in base
For Matilda Abigail, widow of Henry John Adeane.   She d. 28
July 1850. (B.L.G. 1937 ed.)

6. All black background
Adeane arms only, as 3.
Crest: A demi-griffin wings elevated or collared gules   Mantling:
Gules and argent   Motto: Resurgam
Probably for Robert Jones Adeane, who d. unm. 7 Dec. 1853.
(B.L.G. 1937 ed.)

7. Dexter background black
Qly of six, 1st and 6th, Adeane, as 3, 2nd, Whorwood, as 2,
3rd, Bridges, as 2, 4th, Argent a fess between three martlets sable
(Berkeley), 5th, Chandos, impaling, Argent on a saltire azure a bezant
(Yorke)
Crest: As 4.   Mantling: Sable and or   Motto: In coelo quies
For Henry John Adeane, who m. 1860, Elizabeth Philippa, dau. of
Charles, 4th Earl of Hardwicke, and d. 17 Feb. 1870. (B.L.G. 1937 ed.)

BARRINGTON

1. All black background
Argent a chevron sable between three rams' heads erased azure
(Bendyshe)
Crest: From a ducal coronet a talbot's head or   Mantling: Gules
and argent   Motto: Utrâque pallade
Probably for John Bendyshe, d. 1 Nov. 1865.   (M.I.)

BOTTISHAM

1. Sinister background black
Argent on a fess gules three bezants (Jenyns), impaling, Or ermined
sable four fusils in fess vert, on a chief azure an annulet or between two
bezants (Heberden)
Motto: Resurgam   Cherub's heads above
For Mary, dau. of William Heberden, M.D., who m. the Rev. George
Leonard Jenyns, of Bottisham Hall, and d. 18 Aug. 1832, aged 69.
(B.L.G. 5th ed.; M.I.)

2. All black background
Argent on a fess gules three roundels argent (Jenyns), impaling, Ermine
four fusils in fess vert, on a chief azure a crescent sable between two
suns in splendour or (Heberden)
Crest: A demi-lion rampant holding a spearhead or   Mantling:
Gules and or   Motto: Ignavis nunquam   Winged skull below
For the Rev. George Leonard Jenyns, of Bottisham Hall, who d. 25
Feb. 1848, aged 84.   (Sources, as 1.)

CAMBRIDGE
King's College

1. All black background
Vert an arrow in pale argent between two garbs or, on a chief argent
a cherub's head proper between two estoiles of six points or
(Thackeray), impaling, Azure a chevron between three hanks of
cotton argent (Cottin)
Crest: An eagle rising in its beak an arrow argent   Mantling: Vert
and argent   Motto: Nobilitas sola virtus
For the Rev. George Thackeray, Provost 1814–1850, who m. 2nd,
Mary Ann, dau. of Alexander Cottin, of Cheverells, Herts, and d. 20
Oct. 1850. (Alumni Cantabrigienses)

Magdalene College

1. Sinister background black
Qly per pale indented or and azure in the second and third quarters an
eagle displayed or, over all on a bend azure a fret between two martlets
or (Magdalene College), impaling, Or an eagle displayed azure armed
gules surmounted by a lymphad sable, flagged gules, in the dexter
canton a sinister hand gules, in the sinister canton an open book argent
lettered sable bound gules, all within a bordure gules (Donaldson)
Crest: On a rock a raven proper   A small hatchment, c. 2 ft. x. 2 ft.
For the Rev. Stuart Alexander Donaldson, Master 1904–1915, who
d. 29 Oct. 1915. (Alumni Cantabrigienses)

2. Sinister background black
Magdalene College, impaling, Argent a quatrefoil between two trefoils
in bend sable between four bendlets gules (Benson)
Crest: A bear's head erased argent muzzled gules   A small hatchment,
c. 2 ft. x 2 ft.
For Arthur Christopher Benson, Master 1915–1925, who d. unm.
16 June 1925. (Alumni Cantabrigienses)

St. John's College

1. Black only behind arms of Wood
Sable a chief gules over all a lion rampant argent (Wood), impaling, to
dexter, Qly, 1st and 4th, France, 2nd and 3rd, England, all within a
bordure compony argent and azure (St. John's College), and to sinister,
Gules three keys palewise wards upwards or (Deanery of Ely)
Motto: Resurgam
For the Very Rev. James Wood, Master 1815–1839, Dean of Ely
1820–1839, who d. 23 Apr. 1839. (Alumni Cantabrigienses)

CHATTERIS

1. All black background
On a lozenge surmounted by a cherub's head   Qly, 1st and 4th,
Argent on a saltire between three griffins' heads erased sable,
langued gules, and in base a woolpack sable, another saltire or
(Gardner), 2nd and 3rd, Azure on a chevron between two boars' heads
couped in chief and a padlock argent in base a lozenge gules between
two keys in chevron sable (Dunn)   In pretence: Gardner
Motto: Resurgam
For Jane, dau. and heir of John Gardner, who m. William Dunn, who
took the name of Gardner. She d. 25 Mar. 1839.   (M.I.)
(There is another hatchment for Jane Dunn–Gardner at Fordham)

2. Sinister background black
Qly, 1st and 4th, Per pale gules and azure a griffin segreant or, on a
chief ermine three lozenges azure (Chafy), 2nd and 3rd, Gules four
molets two and two or a canton ermine (Westwood), impaling, Or
three candlesticks proper (Kyle)
Crests: Dexter, A cubit arm habited sable holding in the hand proper
a palm branch or   Sinister, A peacock in its pride proper
Motto: Fide et fiducia
Frame inscribed 'To Wm. Westwood Chafy 1873'
For Annette, 2nd dau. of the Rt. Rev. Samuel Kyle, Bishop of Cork,
Cloyne and Ross, who m. 1839, as his 1st wife, William Westwood
Chafy, of Conington House, Cambs, and d. 11 Jan. 1849.
(B.L.G. 7th ed.)

3. All black background
Vert a chevron argent gutty gules between three pheons or (Holman)
Crest: A crossbow erect or between two wings gules   Mantling:
Gules and argent   On scroll below shield: Michael Holman Armg[r]
obiit 19 die Octob. An. Dom. 1673.
On a wood panel   A small hatchment, c. 2½ ft. x 2½ ft.
(This hatchment closely resembles a memorial board, but it has been
included here as the inscription is brief and relates only to the date
of death)

CHIPPENHAM

1. All black background
Argent a lion rampant gules, on a chief sable three escallops argent, a
crescent for difference (Russell), impaling, Russell undifferenced
Earl's coronet   Crest: A goat passant argent attired or
Mantling: Gules and argent   Motto: Che sara sara   Supporters:

Dexter, A lion gules   Sinister, An antelope gules attired or; both
having their forelegs on anchors or   Skull below
For Edward, 1st Earl of Orford, who m. his cousin, Margaret, dau. of
William, 1st Duke of Bedford, and d.s.p. 26 Nov. 1727.   (B.E.P.)

2. Sinister background black

Qly, 1st and 4th, qly i. & iv. Azure a palm branch in bend sinister
between three fleurs-de-lys or (Montgomerie), ii. & iii. Gules three rings
or (Eglinton), 2nd and 3rd, Argent a millrind sable (Turner), impaling,
Or two bars azure each charged with a barrulet dancetty argent, a
chief indented azure (Sawbridge)
For Catherine, dau. of Jacob Sawbridge, who m. 1739, George
Montgomerie, of Chippenham Hall, and d. 28 Dec. 1753.
(B.L.G. 1965 ed.)

3. Dexter background black

Qly, 1st and 4th, Montgomerie, 2nd, Eglinton, 3rd, Turner   In
pretence: Gules semy of bees and three beehives or (Lehoop)
Crest: A palm branch proper   Mantling: Gules and argent
Motto: Procedamus pace   Skull below
For George Montgomerie, who m. 2nd, 1758, Elizabeth, dau. and
co-heir of Isaac Le Heup, and d. 26 Mar. 1766.   (B.L.G. 1965 ed.)

4. Dexter background black

Qly, 1st and 4th, Argent a fess azure fretty or, in chief a lion rampant
gules between two fleurs-de-lys azure in base an anchor sable (Tharp),
2nd and 3rd, Gules on a bend between two lions rampant argent
three parrots sable (Partridge), impaling, Qly, 1st and 4th, Azure three
molets argent within a double tressure flory counterflory or (Murray),
2nd and 3rd, qly. i. & iv. Or a fess chequy azure and argent (Stewart),
ii. & iii. Or two pallets sable (Strabolgi)   In pretence: (over impalement
line)   Gules three legs in armour conjoined or (Isle of Man)
Crest: A demi-woman habited or, mantle purpure, in her right hand an
anchor proper   Mantling: Gules and ermine   Motto: Resurgam
Skull below
For Joseph Tharp, who m. 1788, Susan, dau. of John, 4th Earl of
Dunmore, and d. 1804.   (B.L.G. 1937 ed.)

5. Sinister background black

Tharp, impaling, Azure a chevron argent between three falcons proper
(Phillips)
Motto: Resurgam
For Anna Maria, dau. of Col. Charles Phillips, of Ruxley Lodge, Surrey,
who m. 1796, John Tharp, and d. 16 Dec. 1840.   (B.L.G. 1937 ed.)

6. All black background

Arms: as 5.

Crest, mantling and motto: As 4.
For John Tharp, who m. Anna Maria, dau. of Col. Charles Phillips,
and d. 1 Apr. 1851.   (B.L.G. 1937 ed.)

7. Dexter background black
Qly, 1st and 4th, Tharp, 2nd and 3rd, Partridge
Crest and mantling: As 4.   Motto: In spe spiro
Possibly for John Manners Gordon Tharp, d. 21 Apr. 1875.   (M.I.)
(These hatchments were restored by Lt.-Col. R. L. V ffrench-Blake
in 1981)

CROXTON

1. All black background (should be sinister black)
Argent a chevron azure between three eagles' legs erased each entwined
by a serpent proper (Newton), impaling, Qly, 1st and 4th, Or a fleur-
de-lys azure (Portman), 2nd and 3rd, Gules a chevron between three
cross crosslets argent (Berkeley)
Crest: An eagle's leg and serpent as in the arms   No helm, mantling
or motto
For Mary, dau. of Wyndham Berkeley Portman, of Ham Park, who m.
1852, as his 1st wife, George Onslow Newton, of Croxton Park, and d.
1855.   (B.L.G. 5th ed.)

DULLINGHAM

1. All black background
On a lozenge   Azure a fret argent, on a chief argent three leopards'
faces gules (Jeaffreson)
Motto: Mors janua vitæ
Probably for Sarah Elizabeth Jeaffreson, who d. unm. 11 May 1804.
(B.L.G. 5th ed.)

2. Dexter background black
Jeaffreson, impaling, Vert on a chevron between three stags trippant or
three fleurs-de-lys gules (Robinson)
Crest: A wolf's head erased argent collared or   Mantling: Gules and
argent   Motto: Resurgam
For Lieut.-Gen. Christopher Jeaffreson, of Dullingham, who m. 1794,
Harriet, Viscountess Gormanston, relict of Anthony, 11th Viscount,
and dau. of John Robinson, of Denston Hall, Suffolk, and d. 22 Oct.
1824, aged 63.   (B.L.G. 5th ed.; M.I.)

3. All black background

Two lozenges, one above and partly surmounted the other
1. Or on a fess indented sable three crescents or (Preston), impaling,
Robinson, the lozenge surmounted by a viscountess's coronet
Supporters: Dexter, A lion or   Sinister, A fox proper
2. Azure a fret argent, on a chief argent three leopards' faces sable
(Jeaffreson), impaling, Robinson
For Harriet, formerly Viscountess Gormanston, widow of Christopher
Jeaffreson. She d. 6 Feb. 1826.   (B.L.G. 5th ed.)

4. Sinister background black

Ermine three lozenges in fess sable (Pigott)   In pretence; Jeaffreson
Motto: Resurgam
For Harriet, dau. of Christopher Jeaffreson, who m. as his 1st wife,
1827, William Pigott, J.P., D.L., and d. 12 Mar. 1838.   (B.L.G.
7th ed.)

5. Dexter background black

Pigott   In pretence: Jeaffreson   Also impaling, Azure three
birdbolts or (Boland) (impalement occupies only 1/3 of the shield)
Crest: As 2.   Mantling: Sable and argent   Motto: In coelo quies
For William Pigott, J.P., D.L., who m. 1st, 1827, Harriet, dau. of
Christopher Jeaffreson, of Dullingham, and 2nd, 1847, Charlotte Maria,
dau. of Colonel Boland, and d. 23 Mar. 1875.   She d. 8 Sept. 1884.
(B.L.G. 7th ed.)
(This hatchment, recorded in 1952, is now missing)

FORDHAM

1. All black background

On a lozenge surmounted by a skull   Argent three bars sable
charged with six cinquefoils, three, two and one argent (Dayrell),
impaling, Argent on a bend azure between three choughs proper three
garbs or (Wicksted)   To dexter and sinister, in the angles of the
hatchment, are two small lozenges and above each of these a shield
Dexter lozenge, Sable on a bend between two nags' heads erased
argent three fleurs-de-lys sable (Pepys), impaling, Wicksted   Sinister
lozenge, Argent on a bend sable three swans argent (   ), impaling,
Wicksted   Dexter shield, Wicksted, impaling, Argent a cross engrailed
gules on a chief gules a lion passant guardant or ( )   Sinister shield,
Wicksted, impaling, Gules three escallops or (   )
Motto: Secure vivere mors est
A very small hatchment
For Elizabeth, dau. of John Wickstead, of Cambridge, who m. as his 3rd
wife, Peter Dayrell, of Lillingstone Dayrell, and d.   (Burke's
Commoners, III, 150)

FORDHAM

2. Identical to Chatteris 1.
For Jane, dau. and heir of John Gardner, who m. William Dunn, who
took the name of Gardner. She d. 25 Mar. 1839. (M.I. in Chatteris
church)
(There is another hatchment for Jane Dunn–Gardner at Chatteris)

FULBOURN

1. All black background
Argent on a fess sable a rose argent in chief three molets sable
(Townley), impaling, Argent on a chevron engrailed azure between
three martlets sable three crescents or (Watson)
Crest: On a perch or a hawk close proper beaked and belled or
Mantling: Gules and Argent   Motto: Resurgam
For Richard Greaves Townley, of Fulbourn Manor, who m. 1821,
Cecil, dau. of Sir Charles Watson, 1st Bt., of West Wratting, and d.
5 May 1855. She d. 1856. (B.L.G. 1937 ed.)
(In view of the background this hatchment may have been used
subsequently by his widow)

HINXTON

1. All black background
Two shields   Dexter, Qly, 1st, Azure a lion rampant or crowned
argent (Dayrell), 2nd, Argent a saltire gules between four eagles
displayed azure (Hampden), 3rd, Argent on a chevron azure between
three boars' heads couped sable five cinquefoils or (Agmondesham),
4th, Per pale azure and gules three lions rampant argent (Herbert)
Sinister, Azure a chevron between three lions' heads erased or
langued gules (Windham)
Crests: Dexter, A goat's head argent armed or   Sinister, A lion's
head within a fetterlock or   Mantling: Gules and argent   Motto:
Virtus mille scuta
For Sir Thomas Dayrell, of Shudy Camps, who m. Sarah, dau. and
co-heir of Sir Hugh Windham, Bt., of Pilsden Court, Dorset, and
d. 2 Apr. 1669. (B.L.G. 5th ed.; M.I.)

2. All black background
Qly, 1st and 4th, Dayrell, with crescent for difference, 2nd and 3rd,
Ermine a chevron between three cocks azure wattled gules (Glasscock)
Crest: A goat's head argent armed or   Mantling: Gules and argent

Motto: Virtus mille scuta
Possibly for Marmaduke, 2nd son of Sir Marmaduke Dayrell, who d.
    (M.I.)

3. All black background
On a lozenge surmounted by a cherub's head
Arms: Dayrell only, as 1.
For Sarah, elder dau. of Sir Marmaduke Dayrell, d. 25 Aug. 1728,
aged 46, or her sister, Catherine, d. 1757, aged 70.   (M.I.s)

4. All black background
Two coats per pale, Vert a chevron embattled between three harts
statant or (Green), Per chevron argent and gules a crescent
counterchanged, on a chief gules a unicorn's head erased between two
leopards' faces or (Chapman), impaling, Sable three horses' heads
erased argent (   )
Crest: A stag's head erased argent, attired, murally gorged and chained
or   Mantling: Gules and argent   Motto: Resurgam
Unidentified

5. All black background
On a lozenge   Per pale azure and gules three lions rampant argent
(Herbert), impaling to dexter, Dayrell as 1, and to sinister, Argent on a
chevron gules between three goats' heads erased azure armed and
collared or three lozenges or, on a chief sable a lion passant guardant
ermine (Hinde)
For Barbara, dau. of Anthony Powell, alias Herbert, who m. 1st, Francis
Dayrell, 2nd, Eusebius Andrew, and 3rd, Sir Edward Hinde, of
Madingley, and d. 1667, aged 88.   (M.I.)

6. Dexter background black
Argent a chevron engrailed between three griffins' heads erased sable
ermined or (Raikes), impaling, Raikes
Crest: A griffin's head erased sable ermined or   Mantling: Gules
and argent   Motto: Futuri cautus
For Charles Raikes, of Hinxton, who m. his cousin Eleanor Raikes,
and d.s.p. 16 Feb. 1828.   (B.L.G. 7th ed.; M.I. in churchyard)

7. All black background
On a lozenge surmounted by a cherub's head
Arms: As 6.
Motto: Resurgam
For Eleanor, widow of Charles Raikes, d. 18 Dec. 1830. (Sources, as 6.)

ISLEHAM

1. All black background
Gules on a bend argent three molets sable (Daston)
Crest: A buck's head pierced with an arrow proper   Mantling:
Gules and argent   Motto: Deo volente   Cherubs' heads at sides
of shield and below
For Richard Daston, b. 1 May 1700, d. 23 Feb. 1758.   (M.I.)

KIRTLING

1. Sinister background black
Qly, 1st and 4th, Or a fess chequy argent and azure within a double
tressure flory counterflory gules (Stuart), 2nd and 3rd, Argent a lion
rampant azure (Crichton)   In pretence: Azure a lion passant or
between three fleurs-de-lys argent (North)
Marchioness's coronet   Mantle: Gules and ermine   Motto: Serva
fidem   Supporters: Dexter, A horse argent bridled gules
Sinister, A stag proper
For Maria, dau. of George Augustus, 3rd Earl of Guilford, who m.
1818, John, 2nd Marquess of Bute, and d.s.p. 11 Sept. 1841.
(B.P. 1949 ed.)

2. Sinister background black
Qly, 1st, North, 2nd, Per pale or and azure, on a chevron between three
griffins' heads erased five fleurs-de-lys all counterchanged (Pope), 3rd,
qly. i. & iv. Argent three lozenges conjoined in fess gules a bordure
sable (Montagu), ii. & iii. Or an eagle displayed sable (Monthermer), 4th,
Or an escutcheon between eight martlets, three, two, three sable
(Brownlow)   In pretence: Argent a talbot sejant sable (Furnese)
Countess's coronet   Motto: La vertu est la seule noblesse
Supporters: Two dragons, wings elevated sable ducally gorged and
chained or
For Katherine, Countess Dowager of Rockingham, dau. and co-heir
of Sir Robert Furnese, Bt., who m. 1751, as his third wife, Francis, 1st
Earl of Guilford, and d. 22 Dec. 1766.   (B.P. 1949 ed.)

3. Dexter background black
North, within the Garter   In pretence: Argent two bars azure over
all a double-headed eagle displayed gules (Speke)
Earl's coronet   Crest: A dragon's head couped sable ducally gorged
and chained or   Mantle: Gules and ermine   Motto: La vertu ·
est la seule noblesse   Supporters: Two dragons, wings elevated
proper ducally gorged and chained or   Skull below

For Frederick, 2nd Earl of Guilford, K.G., who m. 1756, Anne, dau.
and heir of George Speke, of White Lackington, Somerset, and d.
5 Aug. 1792.   (B.P. 1949 ed.)

4. All black background
On a shield (should be on lozenge)
North   In pretence: Argent in chief a pheon sable in base a stag's
head couped gules within a bordure embattled azure bezanty (Coutts)
Countess's coronet   Mantle and supporters: As 3.   Motto: In
coelo quies
For Susan, dau. of Thomas Coutts, who m. 1796, as his 2nd wife,
George Augustus, 3rd Earl of Guilford, and d. 24 Sept. 1837.
(B.P. 1949 ed.)

5. Dexter background black
North, impaling, Gules on a chief argent three fireballs proper
(Boycott)   Earl's coronet   Crest: A dragon's head erased proper
ducally gorged and chained or   Mantle and supporters: As 3.
Motto: Animo et fide
For Francis, 4th Earl of Guilford, who m. 1810, Maria, 5th dau. of
Thomas Boycott, of Wrexham, and d.s.p. 11 Jan. 1817. (B.P. 1949 ed.)

6. All black background
On a lozenge   Arms: As 5.
Mantle and supporters: As 3.
For Maria, widow of Francis, 4th Earl of Guilford. She d.s.p. 1821.
(B.P. 1949 ed.; B.L.G. 5th ed.)

7. All black background
North arms only, with badge of Order of St Michael and St George
pendent   Earl's coronet   Mantle and supporters: As 3.
Motto: Animo et fide
For Frederick, 5th Earl of Guilford, who d. unm. 14 Oct. 1827.
(B.P. 1949 ed.)

8. All black background
On a lozenge surmounted by a cherub's head
North arms only
No crest, mantle or coronet   Supporters: As 3.
Possibly for Georgiana, dau. of the 3rd Earl, d. 25 Aug. 1838.
(Source, as 7.)

LANDWADE

1. Dexter background black
Sable a chevron between three griffins' heads erased argent langued

gules, the Badge of Ulster (Cotton), impaling, Argent on a bend sable
between two choughs proper three escallops argent (Rowley)
Crest: A griffin's head erased argent langued gules   Motto: Fidelitas
vincit   Banners and flags in lieu of mantling
For Sir Charles Cotton, 5th Bt., who m. 1798, Philadelphia, dau. of
Sir Joshua Rowley, Bt., and d. 24 Feb. 1812. She d. 5 Apr. 1855.
(B.P. 1949 ed. under Rowley)

2. Dexter background black
Cotton, no Badge of Ulster, and griffins' heads beaked or, impaling,
Argent the base vert arising therefrom three hop-poles sustaining their
fruit all proper (Houblon)
Crest: As 1, with griffin's head beaked or   Motto: As 1.
For the Rev. Ambrose Alexander Cotton, Rector of Girton, who m.
1807, Maria, dau. of Jacob Houblon, of Hallingbury Place, Essex,
and d. 9 Mar. 1846, aged 81.   (B.L.G. 1937 ed. under Houblon)

3. All black background
On a lozenge surmounted by a cherub's head
Arms: As 2.
For Maria, widow of the Rev. Ambrose Alexander Cotton.
She d.   (Source, as 2.)

4. Dexter background black
Cotton, as 2, impaling, to dexter, Argent on a chevron engrailed
azure between three martlets sable three crescents or (Watson), and to
sinister, Gules on a chevron or between three bezants three crosses
formy fitchy sable (Smith)
Crest: As 1.   Mantling: Gules and argent   Motto: Resurgam
For Alexander Cotton, Lieut. R.N., son of the Rev. Ambrose Alexander
Cotton, who m. 1st, 1833, Marianne, dau. of Sir Charles Watson, Bt.,
and 2nd, Henrietta, dau. of the Rev. S. Smith, D.D., Dean of Christ
Church, Oxford, and d. 24 May 1860, aged 51. She d. 19 Oct. 1899,
aged 83. (per P. Spufford)

LEVERINGTON

1. Dexter background black
Azure a chevron between three pheons or, on a chief gules three
maidens' heads couped at the shoulders proper vested azure (Swaine),
impaling, Gules three boars' heads two and one argent between nine
cross crosslets three, three and three or (Taylor)
Crest: A maiden's head couped at the shoulders proper crowned or
Mantling: Gules and argent   Motto: In coelo quies
For Daniel Swaine, who m. Mary, dau. and co-heir of Simon Taylor
of Lynn, and d. 25 Mar. 1782, aged 59.   (M.I.)

2. Dexter background black
Swaine   In pretence: Gules three ? boars' heads erased argent
(Robertson)   Crest and mantling: As 1.   Motto: Resurgam
Probably for Spelman Swaine, only son of John and Alice, who m.
Dorothy, only dau. of Walter Robertson, of Lynn, and d. 29 Oct. 1803.
(M.I.)

3. Dexter background black
Swaine arms only
Crest and mantling: As 1.   Motto: Non omnis moriar
Unidentified

4. All black background
Swaine, with crescent for difference
Crest and mantling: As 1, but no crown   Motto: Nec pietas moram
Palm branches flanking base of shield
Possibly for Spelman, 2nd son of Thomas Swaine, d. 18 Oct. 1761.
(M.I.)

5. All black background
Qly gules and or in the first and fourth quarters a cross potent or
(Cross)   Crest: A stork proper with a cross formy argent in its beak
Mantling: Gules and argent   No motto
Unidentified

LONG STANTON, All Saints

1. All black background (should be dexter black)
Azure a chevron between three garbs or (Hatton), impaling, Qly, 1st
and 4th, Gules a fess ermine between three dolphins or (Ascham),
2nd and 3rd, Azure an eagle displayed argent (Cotton), the Badge of
Ulster over impalement line
Crest: A hind statant or   Mantling: Gules and argent   Motto: In
coelo quies   Winged skull below
For Sir Thomas Hatton, 8th Bt., who m. Harriet, dau. of Dingley
Ascham, of Connington, Cambs., and d. 7 Nov. 1787.   (B.E.B.)

2. All black background
On a lozenge surmounted by a cherub's head
Qly, 1st and 4th, Hatton, 2nd, qly. i. Cotton, ii. Azure a saltire and a
chief or (de Brus), iii. Or three piles gules (Scott), iv. Argent a lion
rampant azure a chief gules (Waltheof), 3rd, Qly, i. Or a lion rampant
within a royal tressure gules (Stewart), ii. & iii. Gules a fess between
three dolphins or (Ascham), iv. Azure a cross flory between four
martlets or (for Goleborne)

Motto: Resurgam
Probably for Frances Hatton, d. 22 May 1838. (M.I.)

3. **Identical to 2.**
Probably for Elizabeth Ann Hatton, d. 1845. (M.I.)

PAMPISFORD

1. **Sinister background black**
Per saltire or and azure four horses' heads couped counterchanged
(Binney), impaling, Argent a fess between three lions rampant gules a
bordure ermine (Willis)
Crest: A barbel surmounted by a bulrush proper   No mantling
Mottoes: Dexter, Bene   Sinister, Virtus tutissima cassis
For Cecilia de Anyers, younger dau. of Capt. Henry Rodolph de
Anyers Willis, of Halsnead Park, Lancs, who m. as his 1st wife, James
Binney, of Pampisford Hall, and d. 25 Mar. 1897.   (Memorial window)

SAWSTON Hall

1. **All black background**
Qly of thirty-two, 1st, Gules fretty argent (Huddleston), 2nd, Argent
a bend between two molets sable (Pyell), 3rd, Per fess argent and gules
six martlets counterchanged (Fenwick), 4th, Argent a lion rampant
sable (Stapleton), 5th, Barry of eight or and gules (Fitzalan), 6th,
Per pale or and vert a cross formy gules (Ingham), 7th, Gules a saltire
argent a label compony argent and azure (Nevill), 8th, Or fretty gules,
on a canton per pale ermine and or a lymphad sable (Nevill), 9th, Gules
a lion rampant or (Bulmer), 10th, Azure an orle within eight cross
crosslets or (   ), 11th, Or a chief dancetty azure (Middleham), 12th,
Qly or and gules a bend sable (Clavering), 13th, Argent three fusils
conjoined in fess gules (Montagu), 14th, Or an eagle displayed vert
(Monthermer), 15th, Gules a cross engrailed argent (Inglethorpe), 16th,
Argent a saltire engrailed gules (Tiptoft), 17th, Azure two chevrons or
(FitzRandolph), 18th, Argent a fess double cotised gules (Badlesmere),
19th, Azure a fess between three leopards' faces or (De La Pole), 20th,
Argent on a canton gules a rose or (Bradston), 21st, Argent on a fess
dancetty sable three bezants (Burgh), 22nd, Or a lion rampant gules
(Charlton), 23rd, Or a lion's gamb erased in bend gules (Powys), 24th,
Azure floretty a lion rampant guardant argent (Holland), 25th, England
within a bordure argent (Holland, Earl of Kent), 26th, Or two bars and
in chief three roundels gules (Wake), 27th, Sable three crescents within
the horns of each a molet argent (Beconsall), 28th, Sable a cross
formy argent (Beconsall), 29th, Argent two chevrons sable between

three chaplets gules (Ashton), 30th, Gules three cinquefoils argent
(Farrington), 31st, Argent a chevron gules between three leopards'
faces sable (Farrington), 32nd, Argent a cross engrailed sable between
four roundels gules (Clayton), impaling, Qly, 1st and 4th, Azure ten
billets, four, three, two, one or, on a chief or a lion rampant issuant
sable (Dormer), 2nd, Gules on a chevron between three chubs naiant or
three martlets sable, on a chief dancetty argent three escallops gules
(Dorre alias Chobbs), 3rd, Argent three fleurs-de-lys azure
(Collingridge)
Crests: (to dexter and sinister of arms which are on a decorative
cartouche)   Dexter, Two arms embowed vested argent holding a
scalp proper   Sinister, On a glove in fess argent a hawk argent
belled or
For Henry Hodelston, of Sawston, who m. Dorothy, dau. of Robert,
1st Lord Dormer, and d. 1657.   (B.L.G. 1937 ed.; M.S. Ped.)
(This hatchment, recorded since the Survey began, is no longer in
the Hall)

2. Sinister background black
Gules a fret argent (Huddleston), impaling, Qly, 1st, Sable a helm with
visor open affronté proper (Bostock), 2nd, Gules a lion rampant argent
(   ), 3rd, Azure a chevron between three molets or (   ), 4th,
Azure a lion rampant or, on a chief argent three molets gules (   )
On a shield suspended from a lover's knot
For Mary, dau. of Richard Bostock, of Wexhall, Salop, who m. Richard
Huddleston, of Sawston, and d. 30 Aug. 1729.   (B.L.G. 1937 ed.)

3. All black background
Qly of six, 1st, Gules fretty argent (Huddleston), 2nd, England within
a bordure argent (Holland, Earl of Kent), 3rd, Gules a saltire argent
a label compony argent and azure, a crescent for difference (Nevill),
4th, Argent three fusils conjoined in fess gules (Montagu), 5th, Or an
eagle displayed vert (Monthermer), 6th, Or a lion rampant gules
(Charlton)
Crest: Two arms embowed vested argent holding a scalp proper
Mantling: Gules and argent   Motto: Soli Deo honor et gloria
Unidentified
(This hatchment is now at Stonor Park, Oxfordshire)

SWAFFHAM PRIOR

1. All black background
On a lozenge surmounted by a cherub's head
Argent a wolf's head erased proper in dexter chief a molet gules (Allix),
impaling, Sable a cross formy fitchy or, a canton argent (Collyer)

For Sarah, dau. of the Rev. William Collyer, Vicar of Swaffham Prior,
who m. 1782, John Peter Allix, of Swaffham Prior House, and d.
He d. 16 May 1807.   (B.L.G. 1937 ed.)

2. Dexter background black
Allix, impaling, Or on a chevron embattled counterembattled argent
between three towers sable three bombs sable fired proper, a chief
azure (Pardoe)
Crest: A wolf's head erased proper   Mantling: Gules and or
Motto: Resurgam   Winged skull in base
For John Peter Allix, who m. 1816, Maria (d. 21 May 1854), dau. of
John Pardoe, of Leyton, Essex, and d.s.p. 19 Feb. 1848.
(B.L.G. 1937 ed.)

3. Dexter background black
Argent a wolf's head erased gules in dexter chief a molet gules, all
within a bordure sable (Allix), impaling, Ermine a bull passant
between three annulets gules (Bevan)
Crest: A wolf's head erased gules   Mantling: Gules and or
Motto: Vincit veritas
For Charles Peter Allix, who m. 1866, Laura Agneta Wellington
(d. 6 Apr. 1922), 2nd dau. of Richard Lee Bevan, of Brixworth Hall,
Northants, and d. 10 June 1921.   (B.L.G. 1937 ed.)

4. No background (close framed)
On a lozenge   Argent a wolf's head erased gules langued sable, in
dexter chief a molet gules, all within a bordure sable (Allix), impaling,
Per pale sable and azure two chevronels engrailed between three cross
crosslets fitchy or (Strutt)
For Hilda, 3rd dau. of Henry, 2nd Baron Belper, who m. 1906,
Charles Israel Loraine Allix, and d. 28 Apr. 1923.   (B.L.G. 1937 ed.)
(This is not a true hatchment in that it was not erected until the 1950s)

TRUMPINGTON

1. All black background
Argent a chevron between three buckets sable hooped and handled or
(Pemberton)   In pretence: Qly, 1st and 4th, Argent three bendlets
sable (   ), 2nd and 3rd, Qly ermine and gules four roses, those
in the first and fourth gules seeded or in the second and third or
seeded gules (   )
Crest: A boar's head erect couped sable   Mantling: Gules and argent
Motto: Quies in coelo   Winged skull below
On wood, with wide frame decorated with skulls, crossbones and
hour glasses
Unidentified

WESTON COLVILLE

1. All black background
Per pale argent and ermine, on a chevron engrailed between three
talbots' heads erased sable three estoiles or, a bordure wavy azure (Hall)
Crest: A talbot's head erased sable collared or harnessed argent
Mantling: Sable and argent   Motto: In coelo quies   Six flags in
saltire behind shield
Probably for Charles Hall, who d. 15 Nov. 1880.   (M.I.)

WHADDON

1. Dexter background black
Two shields   Dexter, within the Garter, Argent on a saltire azure a
bezant (Yorke)   Sinister, within an ornamental wreath, Yorke,
impaling, Qly, 1st and 4th, Gules a fess chequy argent and azure
(Lindsay), 2nd and 3rd, Or a lion rampant gules debruised by a ribbon
sable (Abernethy), all within a bordure azure semy of molets or
Earl's coronet   Crest: A lion's head erased proper collared gules
thereon a bezant   Mantle: Gules and ermine   Motto: Nec cupias
nec metuas   Supporters: Dexter, A lion rampant reguardant or
langued and collared gules the collar charged with a bezant
Sinister, A stag proper attired or collared as the lion   The George
suspended by its ribbon below
For Philip, 3rd Earl of Hardwicke, K.G., who m. 1782, Elizabeth
(d. 26 May 1858), dau. of James, 5th Earl of Balcarres, and d. 18 Nov.
1834.   (B.P. 1949 ed.)
(There is another hatchment for the 3rd Earl at Ridge, Hertfordshire)

WHITTLESFORD

1. All black background
Argent a cross couped between four annulets sable, in chief a crescent
gules (Westley), impaling, Or five bars sable over all a bend gules (   )
Crest: A griffin's head couped or, in its beak a wing sable   Mantling:
Gules and argent
Possibly for Robert Westley, of Whittlesford, who m. Elizabeth (d. 24
Apr. 1734), and d.
(MS of M.I.s, Soc. of Gen.)

ESSEX

by

Christopher Harrold

Great Waltham, Langleys: For Nevill Charles Tufnell, 1935
(Photograph by Mr. Don Price)

INTRODUCTION

In the County of Essex (defined by its 'ancient' boundaries) we have one of the largest collections of hatchments. Over two hundred are described in this volume. My thanks are due to those who, over a period of years, have indicated their whereabouts and in varying degrees recorded their blazons. Where appropriate the work of these contributors is acknowledged in the text.

All hatchments known to me – and several unrecorded ones -- were systematically checked and blazoned in 1973-4. We have included several hatchments which have been lost for one reason or another since the survey began in 1952. For example, those at Alresford were destroyed by fire as was the one at Writtle. The condition of many of those described leaves a lot to be desired. Restoration work has fortunately been carried out in several instances; where the name of the restorer has been established it is gratefully acknowledged. It is to be hoped that this work will continue. Records relating to hatchments are few and far between, for example the hatchments depicted in the painting of the interior of Little Dunmow church (Essex Record Office publication No. 40, *Victorian Essex*) are recorded in *East Anglian* 1864, I, 121 and 1869, III, 310, but they are no longer to be seen. In the Essex Record Office – abbreviated to E.R.O. throughout this volume, followed by the catalogue number – are further descriptions in, for example, T/P132/7 which is a drawing of six hatchments at North Ockendon in 1825 (now there are two only of a later date than the drawing). T/P71 describes no less than eighteen hatchments at Great Baddow where now there are only eight.

We have not included modern interpretations such as those at Bowers Gifford which are in the style of the earliest hatchments, being about 2 ft. 3 in. square. They were placed in the church in 1903 by Sir Duncan Campbell, 3rd Bt., Carrick Pursuivant of Arms. Not included either are armorial paintings on board which predate hatchments; the ones at Tilty and Witham are about 2 ft. square but mounted square not lozengewise. Essex shows the development of the hatchment from the achievement of helmet and gauntlets in Grays parish church and the crested helm in Theydon Mount, through the transition from rectangular to lozenge with the distinctive background. An interesting example can be seen at Pebmarsh where there is both an armorial panel, similar to the one at Tilty, and a hatchment type painting mounted lozengewise, which is blazoned, Sable three bendlets argent (Cooke), impaling, Argent on a chief gules two molets or (St John). There is an inscription to Judith, wife of Thos. Cooke, daughter of Oliver St John who was buried 7 April 1674. Her husband was buried 4 March 1680 so the all black background is not strictly correct. For the earliest examples in the county with the distinctive background on a small early hatchment we have to go to Chigwell where there are several 17th century examples.

Most of the hatchments in the county are of the 18th and 19th centuries. The most recent are for Violet Elizabeth Whitmore, at Orsett, who d. 13 June 1927 (painted by Sir Francis Whitmore), and at Great Waltham for Neil Charles Arthur de Hirzel Tufnell, which was made by the College of Arms in 1936.

In common with many other counties, evidence for the placement of specific hatchments is rare. One belonging to a member of the Bonnell family in Purleigh church in 1936 is the subject of correspondence in the Essex Record Office (E.R.O. T/Z 20/8). E.R.O D/DVv46 is an account rendered by Wm. Perry of Witham for painting a hatchment on the death of Jonathan Josiah Christopher Bullock of Faulkbourne Hall in 1832, but no such hatchment can now be seen. Neither are there any to be seen corresponding to the faculty for moving four hatchments at South Weald in 1867 (E.R.O. D/FC 7/5).

The standard works of genealogy and heraldry have been used in attributing coats of arms and owners of hatchments, but one further work deserves special mention. This is the Elliott Armorial, the lifetime's work of the Rev. H. L. Elliott, Vicar of Gosfield, who died in 1920. This work, in four large manuscript volumes, has rightly been described as 'one of the finest and most complete heraldic records ever compiled'. My thanks are due to the Essex Archaeological Society, in whose care this work is, for making it available to me. My thanks are also due to the staff of the Essex Record Office for their kind co-operation.

Christopher Harrold
6 Bradleigh Avenue, Grays

ALRESFORD

The following seven hatchments were all destroyed by fire in 1971; they had been restored in 1964 by Mr. and Mrs. K. R. Mabbitt.

1. Dexter background black

Ermine three leopards passant in pale sable (Adams), impaling, Argent a chevron between three swans sable (Ilbery)
Crest: A greyhound's head erased ermine   Mantling: Gules and argent   Motto: Ne oublie
Probably for John Adams of Alresford Hall, b. 1735, m. Dorothy Ilbery, and d. 1809.   (Morant, II, 571; E.A., I, 412)

2. All black background

On a lozenge surmounted by a cherub's head
Arms: As 1.
Motto: Resurgemus
For Dorothy, widow of John Adams, d. 1812.   (Source, as 1.)

3. Sinister background black

Paly of six argent and gules, on a chief sable three martlets or, on a canton gules a gold medal of the East India Company (Martin), impaling, Argent a chevron between three martlets sable a bordure engrailed or (Jones)
Motto: Si Deus pro nobis quis contra nos   Skull in base
For Sarah, dau. of Samuel Jones, who m. Capt. Matthew Martin, and d. 6 Jan. 1738, aged 56.   (Morant, II, 189)

4. All black background

Argent three pallets gules, on a chief sable three martlets argent, on a canton gules a gold medal of the East India Company (Martin), impaling, Argent a chevron between three birds sable (Jones)
Crest: A marten salient against a cannon erect all proper
Mantling: Gules and argent   Motto: As 3.   Skull in base
For Capt. Matthew Martin, who d. 20 July 1740.   (Morant, II, 189)

5. All black background

Martin, as 4.
Crest, mantling and motto: As 4.   Skull in base
For Samuel Martin, son of Capt. Matthew Martin and Sarah Jones, d. unm. 16 May 1765.   (Source, as 4.)

6. Dexter background black

Martin, as 4, with crescent for difference
To dexter of main shield, Martin, as 4, impaling, Per fess or and argent
(   ) A.Bl.   To sinister of main shield, Martin, as 4, impaling,
Argent a fess between three bulls' heads couped gules armed sable
(Scofield)   D.Bl.
Crest, mantling and motto: As 4.   Skull in base
For Thomas Martin, son of Capt. Matthew Martin and younger
brother of Samuel Martin, from whom he inherited the manor of
Alresford in 1765. He m. 2nd, Dorothy, dau. of William Scofield, and
d. (between 1772 & 1777)   (E.R.O., per D. C. Jennings;
Morant, II, 189)

7. All black background

On a lozenge   Gules two long bows interlaced in saltire or,
stringed argent, between four bezants each charged with a fleur-de-lys
azure (Rebow), impaling, Martin, as 4.
Mantling: Gules and argent   Motto: In coelo quies   Two cherubs'
heads above
For Mary, dau. of Capt. Matthew Martin, who m. Isaac Lemyng Rebow,
of Wivenhoe Park, Colchester, and d.   Or for Mary, dau. and
co-heiress of Thomas Martin, who m. Isaac Martin Rebow, of Wivenhoe
Park, Colchester, and d. 22 Dec. 1804.   (B.L.G. 2nd ed.)

GREAT BADDOW

1. Sinister background black

Qly, 1st and 4th, Sable a stork proper a bordure argent (Mathew),
2nd and 3rd, Azure in chief two estoiles or (Van Lumputt) a label
argent in chief of 2nd quarter, impaling, Argent three lions passant
guardant in pale gules (Brograve)
Motto: Post funera virtus   Cherub's head above
For Catherine, dau. of Sir Berney Brograve, Bt., who m. William
Mathew, brother of Daniel Mathew, of Felix Hall, Essex, and
d.   (B.L.G. 5th ed.; Franks' Cat. of Bookplates)

2. All black background

Qly, 1st and 4th, Mathew, 2nd and 3rd, Azure two estoiles in fess or
(Van Lumputt), impaling, Brograve
Crest: A stork proper   Mantling: Gules and argent   Motto: In
coelo quies
For William Mathew, who d.
(Sources, as 1.)

3. Sinister background black

Argent a lion passant gules between two bars sable charged with three bezants, two and one, in chief three stags' heads cabossed gules (Parker), impaling, Qly argent and gules in the first quarter a cross flory gules (Crosse)
Motto: Forbear   Shield surmounted by a lover's knot and two cherubs' heads
Probably for Mary, wife of James Parker, who d. 17 Aug. 1855. He d. 16 June 1861.
(Bloom; E.R.O.T/P72/1; M.I.)

4. All black background

Parker   In pretence: Argent on a bend cotised sable three martlets argent (   )   Also impaling, Qly argent and gules in the first quarter a cross flory gules (Crosse)
Crest: From a ducal coronet or a bear's head sable muzzled or
Mantling: Gules and argent   Motto: Forbear
Probably for James Parker, d. 16 June 1861.   (Source, as 3.)

5. Dexter background black

Or an anchor in pale sable (Chappell), impaling, Argent on a pile sable three griffins' heads erased argent (Halsey)
Crest: Father Time proper   Mantling: Gules and argent
Mottoes: (above crest) Mors janua vitæ   (below shield) Importu navigo
Unidentified

6. Dexter background black

Chappell, impaling, Qly, 1st and 4th, Azure a bend counter compony argent and sable between six billets or (Callender), 2nd, Sable a stag's head cabossed argent (Mackenzie), 3rd, Gules three legs in armour embowed and conjoined at the thighs proper (Mace)
Crest and mantling: As 5.   Motto: Importu navigo
Unidentified   (Bloom; E.R.O. T/P72/1)

7. All black background

Sable a hawk proper jessed and belled upon a perch or (Hawker), impaling, Argent two bars and in chief three round buckles sable (Luther)
Crest: A hawk's head erased proper   Mantling: Gules and argent
For Edward Hawker, who m. Jane Luther, and d. 1738, aged 75.
(per Arnold Hawker)

8. Dexter background black

Qly, 1st and 4th, Hawker, 2nd, Luther, 3rd, Or on a bend azure three cinquefoils or (Herris), impaling, Argent a chevron between three lions' heads erased sable langued gules (Hall)

Crest and mantling: As 7.   Motto: In coelo salus   Skull in base
For Edward Hawker, who m. Elizabeth Hall, and d. 25 Oct. 1756,
aged 62.   (Source, as 7.)

(All these hatchments were restored by Mr. and Mrs. K. R. Mabbitt)

BERECHURCH

1. **Sinister background black** (background incorrect if right attribution)
Barry wavy of six azure and ermine, on a chief or a demi-lion issuant
sable, the Badge of Ulster (Smyth), impaling, Qly, 1st and 4th,
Ermine two bars vert (Delaval), 2nd and 3rd, Argent a chevron azure
between three garbs gules (Blake)
Motto: Resurgam   Cherub's head above
Possibly for Charlotte Sophia Delaval, dau. of Mr. Blake, of Hanover
Square, who m. Sir Robert Smyth, 5th Bt., and d. 4 Feb. 1823.
(Essex Rev. xxiv, 178)

2. **All black background** (background incorrect if right attribution)
Arms: As 1.
Crest: An ostrich's head, in the beak a horseshoe proper
Mantling: Gules and argent   Motto: Resurgam
Possibly for Sir Robert Smyth, 5th Bt., d. 12 Apr. 1802, aged 58.
(Source, as 1.)

3. **Dexter background black**
Sable a chevron ermine between three millrinds or, on a chief argent a
lion passant gules (Turner), impaling, Qly, 1st and 4th, Argent on a
chevron between three ? talbots' heads erased sable three fleurs-de-lys
argent (   ), 2nd and 3rd, Azure a chevron ermine between three
rams' heads argent (Ram)
Crest: A lion passant gules holding in the dexter paw a laurel wreath
vert   Mantling: Gules and argent   Motto: Quid fas optare
Unidentified

BIRDBROOK

1. **All black background**
Argent a fess and in chief a lion passant gules (Walford)
Crest: From a mural coronet or an ostrich feather argent
Mantling: Gules and argent   Motto: Sum quod eris   Skull below
For Thomas Walford, D.L., who d. 7 Aug. 1833, aged 80.   (M.I.)

BLACK NOTLEY

1. All black background
On a lozenge surmounted by a skull
Argent on a pile azure between two cross crosslets gules an eagle
displayed argent (Kitchen), impaling, Or on a fess sable between three
chess rooks gules three roses or (Watford)
Lozenge surrounded by scrollwork and griffins' heads
For Mary, dau. of Edwin Watford, who m. 2nd, Capt. Thomas Kitchen,
and d. 16 Dec. 1722. (Morant)
(Restored by Mr. and Mrs. K. R. Mabbitt)

BOBBINGWORTH

1. Dexter background black
Argent on a bend gules between three roundels sable three swans
argent (Clarke), impaling, Vert a chevron between three leopards' faces
or (Fitch)
Crest: A lark close gules, in the beak an ear of wheat or
Mantling: Gules and argent   Motto: In coelo quies   Two cherubs'
heads above and skull below
For Richard Clarke, who m. Anne, sister of Thomas Fytche, of
Danbury, and d. 1770.   (Morant I, 149; E.A., I, 787; V.C.H.)

2. All black background
Clarke arms only
Crest: A lark gules wings expanded or, in the beak an ear of wheat or
Mantling and motto: As 1.   Skull below
For John Clarke, who m. Elizabeth, dau. of Sir R. Haddock, and
d. 1726.   (E.A., I, 787, V.C.H.)

3. Sinister background black
On a lozenge suspended from a ribbon
Qly, 1st and 4th, Gules a chevron between in chief two roses and in
base a fleur-de-lys argent, a crescent in chief of 1st quarter for
difference (Cure), 2nd and 3rd, Or a greyhound courant between two
bars sable (Baker), impaling, Argent on a chevron azure between
three roses slipped and leaved proper three fleurs-de-lys argent (Coope)
Motto: Resurgam
For Joanna, dau. of Thomas Coope, of Oxton, Notts, who m. Capel
Cure of Blake Hall, and d. 3 June 1804, aged 43.
(B.L.G. 5th ed.; M.I.; E.A., II, 1243)

4. All black background
Arms: As 3, but no crescent in 1st quarter

Crest: From a ducal coronet or a griffin's head argent, charged on the neck with a rose gules, between two wings expanded argent
Mantling: Gules and argent   Motto: Spes tutissima coelo
For Capel Cure, who d. 21 Jan. 1820, aged 75.   (Sources, as 3.)

5. Dexter background black
Qly, 1st and 4th, Cure, as 4, 2nd and 3rd, Baker, impaling, Argent six lions rampant or a canton ermine (Cheney)
Crest and mantling: As 4.   Motto: Ung coeur fidele
For Capel Cure, of Blake Hall, who m. 1822, Frederica, dau. of Lt.-Gen. Cheney, of Langley Hall, Derby, and d. 1 Feb. 1878, aged 80. (M.I.)

6. All black background
On a lozenge   Arms: As 5.
For Frederica, widow of Capel Cure. She d. 23 Feb. 1878, aged 76. (Source, as 5.)

BOREHAM

1. Sinister background black
Qly, 1st and 4th, Qly or and azure four fusils conjoined in cross counterchanged (Haselfoot), 2nd and 3rd, Gules on a fess engrailed between three roundels argent each charged with a peacock's head erased proper three mascles azure (Peacock), impaling, Argent a chevron sable between three bulls' heads cabossed gules armed or (Curteis)   Cherub's head above
For Charlotte Curteis, of London, who m. Robert Clare Haselfoot, and d. 3 Apr. 1826.   (M.I.; E.A., IV, 2769; Alumni Cantabrigienses)

2. Sinister background black
Qly, as 1, impaling, Argent a talbot passant and a canton sable (   )
Motto: Resurgam
For Frances, second wife of Robert Clare Haselfoot. She d. 8 June 1843. (M.I.)

3. All black background
Arms: As 2.
Crest (on a knight's helm): A demi-peacock, wings expanded, in the beak a snake proper   Mantling: Gules and argent   Motto: Resurgam
For Robert Clare Haselfoot, who d. 7 July 1849.   (M.I.)

4. Sinister background black
Qly of 12, 1st, Argent two chevronels azure within a bordure engrailed gules (Tyrell), 2nd, Gules a fess between three herons argent (Heron),

3rd, Paly of six argent and azure (Borgate), 4th, Gules on a chevron engrailed argent three dolphins naiant proper (Flamberd), 5th, Argent a cross between four escallops sable (Coggeshall), 6th, Vair a chief gules (Filise), 7th, Argent a chevron azure ( ), 8th, Argent a chevron gules between three pheons reversed sable (Sulyard), 9th, Barry wavy of eight or and azure (Feyreford), 10th, Gules on a chief argent two molets pierced sable (Bacon), 11th, Gules a chevron or between three lions rampant argent (Gooch), 12th, Gules a chevron engrailed between three hounds sejant argent (Hungate), in centre chief the Badge of Ulster   In pretence: Or on a chevron azure between three roses gules stalked and leaved proper two lions passant respectant or (Tyssen)   Supporters: Two Bengal tigers rampant reguardant proper
For Sarah, only dau. and heir of William Tyssen, of Waltham House, co. Herts, who m. 1791, Sir John Tyrell, 1st Bt., and d. 19 Dec. 1825.   (B.P. 1875 ed.)

BRADWELL-JUXTA-COGGESHALL

1. Dexter background black

Azure on a bend between two fleurs-de-lys or a lion passant guardant gules holding in the dexter paw a fleur-de-lys azure (Nolan), impaling, Gules a cross flory argent, on a chief azure three buckles or (Carter)
Crests: Dexter (on a knight's helm), out of a ducal coronet or a fleur-de-lys azure   Sinister, a demi-lion rampant gules langued azure holding a fleur-de-lys azure
Mottoes: (above crests) Leges mos majoram judicia   (below shield) SXONÃ 𝟪𝒔𝜠𝒗.'𝜼·𝟫 Supporters: Two lions gules langued azure
For the Hon. Michael Nolan, K.C., of Geraldstown, co. Meath, Chief Justice of S. Wales, who m. Martha Carter, and d. 27 Dec. 1827, aged 62. She d. 6 Aug. 1865, aged 80.   (M.I.)

BRIGHTLINGSEA

1. Sinister background black

Qly, 1st and 4th, Azure a cross hameçon argent (Magens), 2nd and 3rd, Argent on a mount in base three trefoils issuing vert in chief a gem ring or stoned azure (Dorrien), impaling, Qly, 1st and 4th, Argent a chevron between three ravens proper (Rice), 2nd and 3rd, qly i. & iv. Gules a lion rampant a bordure engrailed or (Talbot), ii. & iii. Argent two chevrons between three trefoils slipped azure (de Cardonnel)
Motto: Resurgam

For Henrietta Cecilia, dau. of George Rice and Cecil, Baroness Dynevor,
who m. Magens Dorrien Magens, and d. 17 Dec. 1829, aged 71.
(B.P. 1875 ed.; M.I.)

2. All black background
Arms: As 1.
Crest: An arm erect proper holding three trefoils slipped vert
Mantling: Gules and argent   Motto: In arduis viget virtus
For Magens Dorrien Magens, d. 30 May 1849, aged 87.
(Sources, as 1.)
(Both hatchments restored by Mr. and Mrs. K. R. Mabbitt in 1974)

GREAT BURSTEAD

1. Sinister background black
Argent two chevronels azure within a bordure engrailed gules (Tyrell),
impaling, Gules a lion rampant guardant or langued gules holding in
the dexter paw a rose slipped proper (Master)
Mantle: Gules and ermine   Motto: Sans crainte   Cherub's head above
For Anne, eldest dau. of the Rev. William Master, Rector of East
Hanningfield, who m. as his second wife, John Tyrell, Esq. of
Hatfield Peverell, and d. 1780. He d. 3 Nov. 1786.   (B.P. 1875 ed.;
E.A., II, 1670; *East Anglian*, 1866, II, 344; M.I.)

2. Sinister background black
Qly, 1st and 4th, Azure two swords erect in chevron argent hilted or
between three covered cups or (Jenner), 2nd and 3rd, Or a fess
between three crescents azure each issuing flames proper (Poe), over
all a label for difference, impaling, Tyrell
Cherub's head above and winged skull in base
Inscription attached to hatchment: 'In memory of Mrs. Jenner, late
Miss Tyrell, ob. 15 Sept. 1805, aet. 44.'
For Mary Anne, dau. of John Tyrell, of Hatfield Peverell, who m. the
Rev. John Jenner, D.D., Rector of Buckland and Midley, in Kent,
and d. 15 Sept. 1805, aged 44.   (B.P. 1875, ed.; inscription attached
to hatchment)

3. All black background
Qly, as 2, impaling, Qly of twelve, 1st, Tyrell, 2nd, Gules a fess
between three herons argent (Heron), 3rd, Paly of six argent and sable
(Burgate), 4th, Gules on a chevron engrailed argent three dolphins
naiant embowed proper (Flamberd), 5th, Argent a cross between four
escallops sable (Coggeshall), 6th, Vair a chief gules (Filise), 7th, Argent
on a chevron sable three escallops argent (Hawkwood), 8th, Argent a
chevron gules (Sulyard), 9th, Barry wavy of eight or and azure

(Fayreford), 10th, Gules on a chief argent two pierced molets sable
(Bacon), 11th, Gules a chevron or between three lions rampant argent
(Gooch), 12th, Gules a chevron engrailed argent between three talbots
sejant proper (Hungate)
Crest: A covered cup or between two swords in saltire argent hilted or
Motto: Resurgam   Two cherubs' heads above, and shield flanked by
sprays of leaves
For the Rev. John Jenner, D.D., who m. Mary Anne, dau. of John
Tyrell, and d   (B.P. 1875 ed.; E.A., IV, 3125)

4. Sinister background black
Sable a chevron or ermined sable between three lions rampant or
(Spitty), impaling, Jenner
Frame inscribed: 'In memory of Mrs. Spitty late Miss Jenner niece to
Sir John Tyrell Bart Ob. 27 September 1813 aet 28 '

CANEWDON

1. Dexter background black
Azure three fishes in pale or (Kersteman), impaling, Argent on a bend
gules three leopards' faces or (Spurgeon)
Crest: A demi-knight (negro) in armour, in his dexter hand an arrow
point downwards proper   Mantling: Gules and argent   Motto:
Resurgam
For Jeremiah Kersteman, who d. 12 Apr. 1789, aged 67. His widow,
Mary, d. 12 Sept. 1801, aged 84.   (M.I.; E.A., III, 2486; E.R.O.,
D/DQS 186)

2. All black background
Kersteman, impaling, Argent a chevron between three trefoils slipped
sable (Frost)
Crest, mantling and motto: As 1.
For Jeremiah Kersteman, who m. Elizabeth Frost, of Boreham, and
d. 1822.   (E.A., and E.R.O., as 1)

CHICKNEY

1. All black background
Qly, 1st and 4th, Argent on a chevron between three pelicans in their
piety azure three cinquefoils or (Cranmer), 2nd and 3rd, Chequy or
and gules, on a fess azure a cinquefoil between two annulets or
(Mounsey), impaling, Cranmer
Crest: A crane's head erased argent beaked gules, pierced through the

back of the neck with an arrow proper, barbed and plumed argent
gorged with a collar azure charged with an ermine spot or   Mantling:
Gules and argent   Motto: Resurgam
For James Powell Mounsey, who m. 1814, Ann, dau. of William Webb,
of Quendon Hall, Essex. She took the name of Cranmer in accordance
with the will of Miss Martha Cranmer in 1813. On her marriage her
husband also assumed the name and arms of Cranmer. She d. 1853. He
d.   (B.L.G. 1937 ed.; E.A., II, 1550)

CHIGWELL

1. All black background
On a lozenge surmounted by a cherub's head
Per chevron embattled or and azure three martlets counterchanged
(Hodgson), impaling, Azure a cross or fretty gules (   )
Motto: Resurgam
For Mary Hodgson, of Bowls, who d. 16 Nov. 1837.   (per Arnold
Fellows; M.I.)

2. Dexter background black
Argent a chevron sable between three molets pierced gules (Denny),
impaling, Argent on a chief embattled sable three molets or (   )
Crest: An eagle's head erased or   Mantling: Gules and argent
A small hatchment, c. 2 ft. x 2 ft.
For Edmund Denny, of Brooke House, who d. 1656. (per Arnold
Fellows)

3. All black background
Sable a chevron ermine between three garbs or (Comyns), impaling,
Argent on a chief embattled sable three molets or (   )
Crest: Two arms embowed holding a garb proper   Mantling: Gules
and argent   A small hatchment, c. 2 ft. x. 2 ft.
For Francis Comyns, of White Hart, who m. Anne, widow of Edmund
Denny, and d. 1696. (per Arnold Fellows)

4. Dexter background black
Argent three bendlets gules, on a canton vert a rowel spur or (Knight)
In pretence: Qly, 1st and 4th, Gules a lion rampant reguardant or
(Powell), 2nd and 3rd, Argent three boars' heads couped sable
(Glodrydd) Also impaling, Vert a chevron between three bucks trippant
or (Robinson)
Crest: A spur, rowel upwards or, between two wings conjoined gules
Mantling: Gules and argent   Motto: Mors janua vitæ   Skull below
For Robert Knight of Barrells, who m. 1st, Martha (d. 27 July 1718),

dau. and co-heiress of Jeremy Powell of Edenthorpe, Salop, and 2nd,
Miss Robinson, and d. 8 Nov. 1744.   (M.I. in Wootton Wawen
church; E.A. III, 2657)

5. Sinister background black

Sable three dexter gauntlets backs affronté or, in centre chief a
crescent for difference (Fane)   In pretence: Or on a chief indented
sable three crescents or (Harvey)
Motto: Mors janua vitæ   Two cherubs' heads above shield, which is
suspended from a ribbon
For Isabella Mary, youngest dau. of Admiral Sir Eliab Harvey, of
Rolls Park, who m. as his 1st wife, 1835, Robert George Cecil Fane,
and d.s.p. 15 Dec. 1838.   (B.P. 1939 ed., Earl of Westmorland)

6. All black background

On a lozenge surmounted by a cherub's head
Harvey, impaling, Ermine two bars gules (Nugent)
For Louisa, dau. and co-heir of Robert, Earl Nugent, who m. 1784,
Admiral Sir Eliab Harvey, and d. 4 Dec. 1841, aged 84. He d. 20
Feb. 1830.
(Burke's Commoners, Vol. II, p. 434; M.I.)
(Husband's hatchment is in Hempstead church)

7. All black background

Qly, 1st and 4th, Or on a fess sable three roundels argent (Bramston),
2nd and 3rd, Gules three fleurs-de-lys argent (Mondeford)   In
pretence, and impaling, Or five fusils conjoined in fess vert (Pennington)
Crest: A lion sejant collared sable, the collar charged with three
roundels argent   Mantling: Gules and argent   Motto: Post funera
virtus
For John Bramston, who m. Mary, dau. and heir of John Pennington,
of Chigwell, and d. 17 Aug. 1718.   (Burke's Commoners, Vol. II,
p. 432)

8. All black background

On a lozenge surmounted by a cherub's head
Argent a fret gules, on a chief or a lion passant azure (Urmston),
impaling,   Gules two scimitars in saltire points upwards argent
hilted or between four roses argent (Lawrence)
Motto: Resurgam
For Elizabeth, dau. of George Lawrence, who m. 1777, James
Urmston, of Chigwell House, and d. 21 Feb. 1842, aged 86. He d. 24
Nov. 1815, aged 65.   (B.L.G. 1937 ed.; M.I.)

9. All black background

On a lozenge surmounted by a cherub's head
Gules two demi-lions passant or (Hatch)   In pretence: Per pale

ermine and sable ermined argent, on a chevron between three fleurs-
de-lys four lozenges all counterchanged (Addington)
Motto: Resurgam
For Wilhamina Caroline Addington, who m. James Hatch, of Clayberry
Hall, Lord of the Manor of Chigwell, and d. 11 Apr. 1822. He d. Dec.
1806, aged, 56.
(M.I. in church and Little Ilford churchyard)
(There is another hatchment for her at Little Ilford)

10. Sinister background black

On a chevron cotised sable between three trefoils slipped vert (Abdy)
In pretence: Qly, 1st and 4th, Gules two demi-lions passant guardant or
(Hatch), 2nd and 3rd, Addington
Motto: In coelo quies   Two cherubs' heads above shield, which is
suspended from a beribboned medallion
For Caroline Elizabeth, eldest dau. of James Hatch, of Clayberry Hall,
Essex, who m. John Rutherforth Abdy of Albyns (who took the
additional name of Hatch), and d. 5 May 1838. He d.s.p. 1 Apr.
1840, aged 61.   (B.P. 1949 ed.)

11. All black background

Per pale indented argent and sable a saltire counterchanged (Scott),
impaling, Argent two bars sable in chief three round buckles azure
(Luther)
Crest: From a crown vallery ermine a cubit arm vested per pale
indented argent and gules cuffed argent holding a roll of paper
proper   Mantling: Gules and argent   Motto: in coelo quies
For William Scott, of Woolston Hall, who m. Katharine, dau. of Thomas
Luther, of Stapleford Tawney, and d. 27 June 1725, aged 72. She d.
16 Oct. 1710, aged 58.   (M.I.)

12. All black background

Scott arms only   To dexter of main shield, Scott, impaling, Or
two bars and a chief indented gules (Hare) A.Bl.   To sinister of
main shield, Scott, impaling, Sable a chevron between three roses
argent each charged with a saltire sable (   ) D.Bl.
Crest: From a crown vallery a mailed cubit arm, the hand grasping a
scroll, all proper   Mantling: Gules and argent   Motto: Bona
fide et veritate
For Thomas Scott of Woolston Hall, who m. 1st, Ann Hare, and d. 19
Feb. 1732, aged 52.   (M.I.; Berry's Kent Genealogies)

13. All black background

On a lozenge surmounted by a cherub's head
Argent three lions' heads erased gules (Scott), impaling, Vert ten
escallops four, three, two and one argent (Stonehewer)
Motto: Resurgam

For Dorothy Stonehewer, who m. William Scott of Austin Friars, and d.   (per Arnold Fellows)

14. Dexter background black

Qly of ten, 1st, Per pale azure and gules, on a fess argent between three chessrooks or three escallops gules (Bodle), 2nd, Per pale indented argent and sable a saltire counterchanged (Scott), 3rd, Gules crusilly or three boars' heads couped argent (Swinburne), 4th, Per fess gules and argent three cinquefoils counterchanged within a bordure compony argent and azure (Swinburne), 5th, Vert a lion rampant argent (   ), 6th, Azure a voided escutcheon or (Bartrum), 7th, Gules a fess cotised between two frets or (Drax), 8th, Gules semy of roundels a lion rampant argent (Hewick), 9th, Per pale sable and ermine a fess counterchanged (   ), 10th, Ermine an arbalaster gules (Arblaster), impaling, Argent on a bend cotised gules three bezants (Bishop)

Crest: A boar's head per pale argent and gules, langued gules, charged with a chessrook or   Mantling: Gules and argent   Motto: In bona fide et veritate

For Robert Bodle, of Woolston Hall, who m. Mary Bishop, and d. 4 Aug. 1851, aged 82. She d. 13 Dec. 1854, aged 80. (per Arnold Fellows; E.A., I, 240; E.R.O. T/P196)

15. All black background

On a lozenge (oval) surmounted by a cherub's head and flanked by branches   Qly of ten, as dexter of 14, but 8th quarter, Gules a lion rampant between eight roundels argent (Hewick)

For Mary Elizabeth Bodle, dau. and co-heiress of Robert Bodle. She d. 20 Mar. 1872, aged 76. (per Arnold Fellows)

16. Dexter background black

Argent a chevron between three roses gules barbed proper in chief a molet for difference (Wedderburn)   In pretence: Vert on a chevron argent between in chief two garbs argent banded gules and in base an eagle displayed or three molets vert (   )

Crest: An eagle's head erased proper charged on the neck with a molet argent and above a label bearing the words 'Non degener'   Mantling: Gules and argent   Motto: Aquila non captat muscas

For John Wedderburn, of Woodlands, who d. 1820. (per Arnold Fellows)

17. All black background

Argent issuant from a mount in base vert three gillyflowers stalked and leaved proper, on a chief azure four molets of six points or, a crescent for difference (Sperling)

Crest: Between two wings conjoined at the base and displayed argent a molet of six points or   Mantling: Gules and argent   Motto: Mors janua vitæ

For Henry Sperling, of Fulhams Farm, who m. Elizabeth, dau. and heir
of Thomas Foxall, of London, and d. 27 Sept. 1766. (per Arnold
Fellows; E.A., III, 2528).

CHINGFORD, SS Peter and Paul

1. Dexter background black
Qly, 1st, Argent two bars azure over all a bend sable (Legh), 2nd, Or
three lozenges azure (Baguley), 3rd, Ermine on a chief dancetty gules
three ducal coronets or (Corona), 4th, Argent a fleur-de-lys sable
(Levenshulme)
Crest: A bear passant sable collared and bridled or   Mantling:
Gules and argent   Motto: In coelo quies
Possibly for Robert Leigh, who d. c. 1700 (V.C.H.; P.C.C. Wills)

2. All black background
On a lozenge   Argent a sealion azure langued gules finned and ducally
crowned azure, in chief the Badge of Ulster (Silvester), impaling,
Sable a lion rampant reguardant argent (   )   Cherub's head above
For Harriet, dau of the Rev. Owen Davies, of Southampton, who m.
1793 Sir John Sylvester, Bt. (cr. 1815), and d.   He d. 30 Mar.
1822.   (B.E.B.)

3. Dexter background black
Argent on a canton sable a lion's gamb erased in bend or (Boothby),
impaling, Argent three dung-forks palewise points upwards sable
(Worthington)
Crest: A lion's gamb erased or   Mantling: Gules and argent
Motto: Mors janua vitæ
For Thomas Boothby, who m. Frances Worthington, and d. 13 May
1735.   (M.G. and H., 5th Ser. Vol. I)

4. All black background
Boothby arms only
Crest and mantling: As 3.   Motto: In coelo quies   Two cherubs'
heads above
Possibly for Robert Boothby, of Friday Hill House, who d. 11 Oct.
1774.   (E.A., I, 1003)

5. All black background
Vert a dexter hand clenched couped at the wrist proper (Feast)
Crest: From a ducal coronet or an eagle displayed sable crowned or
Mantling: Gules and argent   Motto: In coelo quies   Skull below
Unidentified

6. All black background
On a lozenge surmounted by two cherubs' heads   Argent two
chevrons gules each charged with a molet argent (Moyer)
Possibly for Catherine, dau. of Laurence Moyer, d. 1724, aged 32.
(E.A., II, 1671)

7. Sinister background black
Gules three cinquefoils argent, in chief two molets in pale argent all
within a bordure engrailed ermine (Hamilton)   In pretence: Gules
three crescents argent a canton ermine (Cooke)
Unidentified

8. All black background
Argent on a chevron sable three garbs or (Newton)
Crest: A man in armour proper, crowned and belted or, facing to the
dexter, kneeling on the sinister knee, the dexter hand in a gauntlet
holding a sheathed sword palewise, hilt upwards or
Mantling: Gules and argent   Motto: Resurgam
Unidentified   (E.A., II, 1505)

(All these eight hatchments are in bad condition and in need of
restoration)

All Saints

1. Sinister background black
Argent on a canton sable a lion's gamb erased in bend or armed gules
(Boothby), impaling, Argent a lion passant gules, on a chief sable
three battleaxes palewise blades to the dexter or (Jackson)
Motto: Post funera virtus   Cherub's head below
For Sarah, dau. of Samuel Jackson, who m. Robert Boothby, and
d.   He d. 1 Dec. 1733, aged 68.   (B.E.B.; M.I.)

2. All black background
On a lozenge surmounted by a cherub's head
Azure a dexter hand clenched couped at the wrist proper (Feast),
impaling, Or a fess between three lions' heads erased sable langued
gules (   )
Motto: In coelo quies   Skull below
Unidentified

(Hatchments restored by Mr. W. Foster–Davis in 1947)

COGGESHALL

1. Dexter background black
Argent a chevron between three eagles' heads erased azure (Honywood),

impaling, Argent a chevron between three roses gules barbed and
seeded proper (Phelips)
Crest: A wolf's head erased ermine   Mantling: Gules and argent
Motto: In coelo quies
For William Philip Honywood, who m. Frances Emma, dau. of Charles
Phelips, of Briggins Park, and d. 28 Feb. 1859. She d. 30 Jan. 1895.
(B.P. 1939 ed.)

COLCHESTER, Castle Museum

1. All black background
Gules a chevron ermine between three bulls' heads cabossed argent
armed or (Bullock)   In pretence: Per pale argent and gules a
cross engrailed counterchanged in dexter chief a cinquefoil gules (Lant)
Crest: Five Lochaber axes proper bound with a cord tasselled or
Mantling: Gules and argent   Mottoes: (above the crest) Nil conscire
sibi (beneath the shield) Esperance en Dieu
For John Bullock, the last male heir of the Bullocks of Faulkbourne,
who m. 1763, Elizabeth Lant, and d.s.p. 1809.
(E.A. II, 1294; inscription by hatchment)

2. Dexter background black
Qly, 1st and 4th, Gules a lion rampant a bordure engrailed argent
(Gray), 2nd and 3rd, Barry of six gules and argent per pale indented
counterchanged (   ), impaling, Argent three bends wavy azure
(Wilbraham)
Crest: A scaling ladder proper   Mantling: Gules and argent
Motto: In coelo quies
For Charles Gray, F.R.S., M.P. for Colchester, who m. 2nd, Mary
Wilbraham, and d. 12 Dec. 1782, aged 86.   (Inscription below
hatchment)

3. All black background
On a lozenge   Sable a lion rampant or between three molets argent
(Webster), impaling, Azure three fishes hauriant argent finned gules
(Kersteman)
Mantling: Gules and argent
For Mary (Kersteman), mother-in-law of Charles Gray, who m. John
Webster, merchant, and d. 1754, aged 92.
(Inscription below hatchment)

St James

1. Sinister background black
Gules a fleece proper banded or between three bees or (Boggis),

impaling, Argent three ravens sable in chief a trefoil slipped azure (Rolfe)
Mantling: Gules and argent   Cherub's head above
Inscribed on frame 'Ann Boggis ob. 1794'
For Ann, dau. of William Rolfe, of Langenhoe Hall, who m. Isaac Boggis, Hamburg merchant, and d. 1794.   (per J. Bensusan–Butt; inscr. on hatchment)
(Restored by Mr. and Mrs. K. R. Mabbitt, 1974)

2. All black background
Gules a fleece proper banded or between three bees or (Boggis), impaling, Argent three ravens sable (Rolfe)
Crest: A cornucopia erect proper   Mantling: Gules and argent
Motto: In coelo quies
Inscribed on frame 'Isaac Boggis, ob. 1801'
For Isaac Boggis, who d. 1801.   (Sources, as 1.)

3. Dexter background black
Qly, 1st and 4th, Argent on a chevron sable three annulets argent (Round), 2nd and 3rd, Qly argent and azure in chief two sinister hands couped erect and in base two human legs couped above the knee erect counterchanged, in fess point a human heart gules (Creffield), in centre chief a crescent for cadency, impaling, Argent three cinquefoils sable (Borthwick)
Crest: A lion couchant argent   Mantling: Gules and argent
Motto: Esse quam videri
For George Round, High Sheriff of Essex, 1845, who m. 1824, Margaret, dau. of Maj.-Gen. W. Borthwick, of Dedham, and d. 1857. (B.L.G. 5th ed.)

Holy Trinity

1. Sinister background black
Sable a chevron wavy between three eagles displayed or (Shawe), impaling Sable a chevron between three trefoils slipped argent (Lewis)
Crest: A hart's head transfixed through the neck by an arrow proper
Mantle: Gules and argent
For Thamar, dau. of Samuel Lewis, of Royden, Suffolk, who m. Sir John Shawe, Recorder of Colchester, and d. 13 Jan. 1681.
(per J. Bensusan–Butt)

2. All black background
Arms: As 1.
Crest and mantling: As 1.
For Sir John Shawe, who d. 1690, aged 73.   (per J. Bensusan–Butt)

3. All black background
Gules on a chief argent two molets sable in fess point the Badge of
Ulster (Bacon)
Crest: A boar passant ermine   Mantling: Gules and argent
Motto: In coelo quies
For Sir Richard Bacon, 7th Bt. of Redgrave and 8th Bt. of Mildenhall,
who d.s.p. 1773, and was buried at Holy Trinity, 11 Apr. 1773.
(B.P. 1878 ed.; per J. Bensusan–Butt)

4. All black background
Argent on a pale sable three roses argent seeded or a crescent on a
crescent for difference (Talcott)
Crest: A demi-griffin argent collared sable, the collar charged with
three roses argent, charged on the shoulder with a crescent on a
crescent for difference   Mantling: Gules and argent
Probably for T. Talcott, who d. 22 Feb. 1685/6.   (M.I.)

5. Dexter background black
Argent a lion statant guardant gules, on a chief sable three stirrups
leathered or (   ), impaling, Gules a fess between two chevrons argent
(Nourse)
Crest: A demi-lion holding a stirrup leathered or   Mantling: Gules
and argent
Unidentified

(These five hatchments have all been restored by Mr. J. Robinson)

COPFORD

1. All black background
Qly, 1st and 4th, Sable two bars ermine between six molets of six
points, three, two and one or (Harrison), 2nd and 3rd, Argent three
crescents paly azure and gules (Haynes)
Crest: A stork wings expanded proper   Mantling: Gules and argent
Motto: Ferendo et feriendo
Probably for Thomas Haynes Harrison, d. 9 May 1895.
(B.L.G. 1937 ed.)

DEDHAM

1. Sinister background black
Or two bars azure, on a canton argent a chaplet gules (Holmes),
impaling, Argent a greyhound courant sable between three choughs
proper (Williams)

Motto: Resurgam   Cherubs' heads and lovers' knot above
For Charlotte Isabella, dau. of Stephen and Charlotte Williams, who
m. the Rev. Gervas Holmes, Rector of Copford, and d. 7 Mar. 1816,
aged 33.   (M.I.)

2. All black background
Gules on a fess between three water bougets argent a cross formy sable
charged with five bezants between two cloves sable (Merry)
Crest: The top of a ship's mast, on a yard sail furled, from the round
top issuing three arrows on each side points upwards, all proper
Mantling: Gules and argent   Motto: Resurgam
For Anthony Merry, of Dedham House, d. 14 June 1835, aged 79.
(M.I.)

GREAT EASTON

1. All black background
Qly, 1st, Argent a chevron azure between three sinister hands couped
gules (Maynard), 2nd, Argent two chevronels sable, on a canton sable
an eagle displayed argent (Pearson), 3rd, Argent a fess nebuly between
three estoiles gules (Everard), 4th, Argent a cross flory sable
(Banaster)
Baron's coronet   Crest: A stag statant proper   Mantling: Gules
and argent   Motto: Manus justa nardus   Supporters: Dexter, A
stag proper attired or   Sinister, A talbot argent pied sable plain
collared gules
For Henry, 4th Baron Maynard, d. 7 Dec. 1742; or for Grey, 5th
Baron Maynard, d. 27 Apr. 1745; or for Charles, 6th Baron Maynard,
d. 30 June 1775. (B.E.P.)

ELSENHAM

1. Dexter background black
Qly gules and argent, on a fess engrailed per pale azure and or,
between three horses courant counterchanged, three roundels
counterchanged (Rush), impaling, Rush
Crest: A wyvern's head erased proper gorged with a collar or charged
with three roundels gules   Mantling: Gules and argent
Motto: Un dieu, un roi, une foi
For George Rush, of Elsenham Hall, who m. 1810, Clarissa, dau. of
Sir William Beaumaris Rush, and d. 10 May 1851, aged 66. She d. 14
Jan. 1876, aged 89.
(B.L.G. 5th ed.; M.I.)

FINCHINGFIELD

1. All black background

Argent a chevron between three roses gules barbed and seeded proper
a crescent for cadency (Ruggles), impaling, Sable three lions passant
in pale argent (English)
Crest: A tower or with flames issuant proper, behind the tower six
arrows in saltire points downwards proper   Mantling: Gules and
argent   Motto: Quies non est sed in coelo
On frame: Sapere aude
For Samuel Ruggles, who m. Sarah English of Bocking, and d. 15
Feb. 1828.   (Burke's Commoners; family tree)

2. Dexter background black

Ruggles, impaling, Argent a chevron or ermined sable between three
molets gules (Freeland)
Crest and mantling: As 1.   Motto: Resurgam
For Thomas Ruggles, of Spains Hall, who m. 2nd, 1799, Jane Anne,
dau. of John Freeland, of Cobham, Surrey, and d. 17 Nov. 1813,
aged 68.   (B.L.G. 1937 ed.; M.I.)

3. Dexter background black

Qly, 1st and 4th, Ruggles, 2nd and 3rd, Gules a cross argent between
four frets or all within a bordure sable charged with eight cinquefoils
argent (Brise), impaling, Azure two bars ermine between six molets
of six points three, two and one or (Harrison)
Crest, mantling and motto: As 2.
For John Ruggles-Brise, of Spains Hall, who m. 1824, Catherine,
dau. of John Haynes Harrison, of Copford Hall, and d. 24 Sept. 1852.
(Sources, as 2)

GESTINGTHORPE

1. Dexter background black

Argent on a chevron ringed at the point between three crescents sable
three roundels argent (Walker), impaling, Or a chevron sable gutty
gules between three crows proper (   )
Crest: A dragon's head vert crowned with an Eastern crown or
Mantling: Gules and argent   Motto: I know that my Redeemer liveth
Skull below
Probably for George Walker, who d. 29 May 1848, aged 58. His widow,
Stephana, dau. of Stephen Round, of Sunningdale, d. 1867.
(M.I.; Essex Rev. LVII, 131)

GOSFIELD

1. Sinister background black
Argent three roses gules barbed and seeded proper a chief gules
(Sparrow), impaling, Gyronny of eight or and sable, on a chief sable
two leopards' faces or (Crowe)
Mantling: Gules and argent   Cherub's head above
For Anne, youngest dau. and co-heiress of James Crowe, of Lakenham,
Norfolk, who m. as his 1st wife, James Goodeve Sparrow, of Gosfield
Place, and. d. 24 Jan. 1813, aged 31.   (M.I.)

2. Sinister background black
Sparrow, impaling, Argent a saltire engrailed between four escallops
sable (Beridge)
Motto: In solo Deo salus   Two cherubs' heads above
For Dorothy, eldest dau. of the Rev. B. B. Beridge, Rector of Algerkirk,
Lincoln, who m. as his 2nd wife, James Goodeve Sparrow, of Gosfield
Place, and d. 12 Feb. 1833, aged 38.   (M.I.)

3. All black background
Sparrow   In pretence: Crowe   Also impaling, Beridge
Crest: From a ducal coronet or a unicorn's head argent armed and
crined or   Mantling: Gules and argent   Motto: In solo Deo salus
For James Goodeve Sparrow, of Gosfield Place, who d. 3 Oct. 1838,
aged 69.   (M.I.)

4. Sinister background black
Two shields, the dexter overlapping the sinister   Dexter, within
the Garter, Qly, 1st, Azure on a cross argent five roundels gules
(Grenville), 2nd, qly, i. & iv. Or an eagle displayed sable (Leofric,
Earl of Mercia), ii. & iii. Argent two bars sable each charged with
three martlets or (Temple), 3rd, Gules two lions passant guardant or
(   ), 4th, Ermine two bars gules (Nugent)   Sinister, within an
ornamental wreath, as dexter with, in pretence, Ermine two bars
gules (Nugent)
Marchioness's coronet   Motto: Templa quam dilecta   Supporters:
Dexter, A lion rampant per fess embattled or and gules
Sinister, A horse argent charged with five eagles displayed sable
For Mary Elizabeth, dau. of Robert, Earl Nugent, who m. 1775,
George, 3rd Earl Temple, K.G. (cr. Marquess of Buckingham
1784), and d. 16 Mar. 1812.   (B.P. 1949 ed.)

HATFIELD PEVEREL

1. All black background
Qly, 1st and 4th, qly. i. & iv. Argent a lion rampant and in the dexter

base a millrind sable (Champion de Crespigny), ii. & iii. Argent three
bars azure (Vierville de Vierville), 2nd and 3rd, Gules a fleur-de-lys or
a canton ermine (Clarke), over all the Badge of Ulster, impaling, Gules
crusilly or a saltire argent (Windsor)
Crests: 1. On a chapeau gules and ermine a cubit arm in armour,
the hand in a gauntlet grasping a scimitar proper, hilted or   2. From a
ducal coronet or a bull's head proper armed or   Mantling: Or and
argent   Motto: In coelo quies
For Sir William Champion de Crespigny, 2nd Bt., who m. 1786,
Sarah, dau. of Other, 4th Earl of Plymouth, and d. 28 Dec. 1829.
She d. 22 Dec. 1825.   (B.P. 1949 ed.)

HEMPSTEAD

1. Dexter background black
Two shields   Dexter, within the Order of the Bath, Or on a chief
indented sable three crescents argent (Harvey)   Sinister, Per pale
or and ermine two bars couped gules (Nugent)
Crest: A dexter hand proper surmounted by a crescent inverted
argent and the legend 'Temeraire'   Mantling: Gules and argent
Motto: Redoutable et fougueux   Supporters: Dexter, A triton
carrying a trident wreathed with laurel, all proper   Sinister, A
horse rampant argent gorged with a naval crown or bearing the
legend 'Trafalgar' and suspended therefrom the Trafalgar medal
For Admiral Sir Eliab Harvey, M.P., G.C.B., of Rolls Park, Chigwell,
who m. Louisa, youngest dau. and co-heir of Robert, Earl Nugent,
and d. 20 Feb. 1830.   (Burke's Commoners)
(Printed on back of original canvas 'Charles Roberson & Co.,
51 Longacre'. Restored by Sir Francis Whitmore in 1958; Lady Louisa
Harvey's hatchment is at Chigwell)

HENHAM

1. All black background
Sable a fess dancetty or in chief three fleurs-de-lys argent (Feake)
In pretence: Sable ermined or a saltire azure between four eagles
displayed gules (Hampton)
Crest: Out of a ducal coronet or a demi-ostrich wings expanded
argent charged on the breast with an annulet gules, in the beak an
inverted horseshoe or   Mantling: Gules and argent   Motto:
Virtutem coelum munerat   Skull below
For Samuel Feake, who m. Anne, dau. and heir of John Hampton, of
Hampden, and d. 16 June 1757. She d. 10 May 1723, aged 34.   (M.I.)

2. All black background
Qly, 1st and 4th, Feake, with an annulet gules in fess point, 2nd and
3rd, Hampton
Crest and mantling: As 1.   Motto: Fama superstes erit   Skull below
For Samuel Feake, of Durrington, who d. unm. 30 Oct. 1774,
aged 63.   (M.I.)

3. All black background
On a lozenge surmounted by a cherub's head   Feake arms only
For Mary Feake, dau. and co-heiress of Samuel Feake. She d. 14 Apr.
1803, aged 82.   (M.I.)

4. Sinister background black
Per chevron or and azure in chief two escallops azure in base a cross
flory argent (Cruse)   In pretence: Qly, 1st and 4th, Feake, as 2,
2nd and 3rd, Hampton
Motto: Resurgam   Two cherubs' heads above shield
For Anne Charlotte Feake, who m. Jonathan Cruse, and d. post 1790.
(M.I.)

(All these four hatchments were restored by Mr. E. B. A. Everett)

HEYBRIDGE

1. Dexter background black
Gules on a bend argent a cinquefoil between two lions passant gules
(Hering)', impaling, Or a boar's head couped gules langued sable
between three water-bougets sable, all within a bordure sable charged
in chief and in base with three padlocks, two and one or, and in the
flanks with two swords erect proper hilted or (Ross)
Crest: An arm in armour embowed proper, the hand holding a dagger
argent hilted or   Mantling: Gules and argent   Mottoes: (above
crest) Arma tuentur pacem   (below shield) Fortitudine non vi
Possibly for Julines Hering, who d. 20 Aug. 1773, aged 81.   (M.I.)

HORHAM Hall, nr. Thaxted

1. Identical to hatchment No. 9 at Theydon Mount
For Sir Thomas Smijth, 8th Bt., who d. unm. 5 Oct. 1833; or for Sir
John Smijth, 9th Bt., who d. unm. 9 Dec. 1838.   (B.P. 1949 ed.)

GREAT HORKESLEY

1. Dexter background black
Sable a chevron engrailed between three garbs or (Kelso)   In pretence:
Qly, 1st and 4th, Azure on a fess argent between three mascles or three

cinquefoils azure (Purvis), 2nd and 3rd, Azure a fess between three
dolphins embowed argent (Leman)
No helm   Crest: A garb or   Motto (above crest): Otium cum
dignitate   Supporters: Two lions rampant gules langued azure each
charged on the shoulder with a garb or
For Edward John Francis Kelso, of Horkesley Park, who m. 1841,
Frances Laetitia Philippa, only child and heiress of Barrington Purvis,
of Beccles, Suffolk, and Purvis Hall, Essex, and d. 26 Oct. 1857.
(B.L.G. 1937 ed.; E.A., III, 2303)

2. All black background
On a lozenge   Kelso   In pretence: Qly, 1st, Purvis, 2nd, Sable a
cross potent or (Allen), 3rd, qly i. & iv. Sable a chevron between
three owls argent, on a chief or three roses gules (Oldham), ii. Gules a
chevron engrailed ermine between three herons proper (Child),
iii. Sable three lions passant guardant argent (   ), 4th Azure a fess
between three dolphins embowed argent (Leman)
Supporters: As 1.
For Frances Laetitia Philippa, widow of Edward John Francis Kelso.
She d. 24 Feb. 1873.   (Sources, as 1.)

3. Dexter background black
Sable two swords in saltire points upwards argent hilts and pommels
or between four fleurs-de-lys or (Barrow), impaling, Argent three
battleaxes sable (Gibbs)
Crest: A demi-figure habited and hatted sable, ruffed argent, carrying a
sheaf or   Mantling: Sable and or   Motto: In coelo quies
Skull in base
Unidentified

4. Sinister background black
Gules between two pillars argent the Blessed Virgin standing with arms
extended, vested, holding in her right hand an ancient church, all
proper; in base three legs in armour, flexed and conjoined in pairle
proper garnished and spurred or (See of Sodor and Man), impaling,
Azure a cross flory or (Ward)   The shield surmounted by a bishop's
mitre
For the Rt. Rev. William Ward, D.D., rector of Great Horkesley,
1817–1838, Bishop of Sodor and Man, 1828–1838. He d. 26 Jan. 1838,
aged 75.   (Wilson, An Island Bishop, S.P.C.K., 1931)

LITTLE ILFORD

1. All black background
On a lozenge   Or a cross flory between four escallops sable (   )
Motto: Resurgam
Unidentified

2. All black background
On a lozenge surmounted by a cherub's head
As 1, impaling, Gules a fess between three crescents or, a canton or
ermined sable (   )
Motto: Resurgam
Unidentified

3. All black background
On a lozenge   Gules two lions passant, hind legs erased or (Hatch)
In pretence: Per pale or ermined sable and sable ermined or, on a
chevron between three fleurs-de-lys four lozenges all counterchanged
(Addington)
Motto: Resurgam
For Wilhamina Caroline Addington, who m. James Hatch, of Chigwell,
and d. 11 Apr. 1822.   (M.I. in churchyard)
(There is another hatchment for her at Chigwell)

4. All black background
Qly, 1st and 4th, Or a lion rampant and a chief gules (   ), 2nd and
3rd, qly i. & iv. Paly of six or and azure (   ), ii. & iii. Or a cockatrice
sable (   ), impaling, Or on a chevron between three horns sable
three cross crosslets or (   )
On a wood panel not canvas
Unidentified

LAMBOURNE

1. All black background
Qly, 1st and 4th, Argent a fess between three martlets sable
(Lockwood), 2nd and 3rd, Ermine on a bend engrailed sable three
roundels argent (Cutts), impaling, Argent a fret sable (Vernon)
Crest: On the stump of an oak tree branched and leaved proper a
martlet sable   Mantling: Gules and argent   Motto: Resurgam
For Richard Lockwood, b. 1672, who m. Matilda, dau. of George
Vernon, of Sudbury, Derbyshire, and d. 31 Aug. 1756. She d. 25 Nov.
1743, aged 54.   (Burke's Commoners; M.I.)

2. All black background
Qly, 1st, Lockwood with label for difference, 2nd and 3rd, Cutts, 4th,
Lockwood, no label, impaling, Qly, 1st, Barry of four argent and
azure a chief sable (Vernon), 2nd and 3rd, Or on a fess azure three
garbs or (Vernon), 4th, Argent a fret sable (Vernon)
Crest, mantling and motto: As 1.
For Richard Lockwood, of Dews Hall, b. 1712, who m. his cousin,
Anna Catherina Vernon, and d.s.p. 25 Mar. 1797. She d. 31 May
1757, aged 47.   (Burke's Commoners; M.I.)

3. All black background
Qly, as 1.
Crest and motto: As 1.   Mantling: Sable and argent
Unidentified

4. All black background
On a lozenge   Qly, as 1.
Mantle: Gules and argent   Motto: Resurgam   Cherub's head
above
Unidentified

5. All black background
A shield and a lozenge   Shield, Argent a fess between three martlets
sable (Lockwood)   Lozenge, Sable a fess dancetty or between
three crescents argent (Rous), impaling, Ermine an eagle displayed
gules armed and langued azure (Bedingfield), the Badge of Ulster over
impalement line
Crests: (above shield) On the stump of an oak tree branched and leaved
proper a martlet sable   (above lozenge) A bay tree proper
Mottoes: (below shield) Mors janua vitæ   (below lozenge) Je vive
en espoir
For the Rev. Edward Lockwood, who m. as his third wife, Judith,
widow of Sir John Rous, Bt., and dau. of John Bedingfield, of Beeston,
Norfolk, and d. 2 Jan. 1802. She d. 10 Sept. 1794.
(Burke's Commoners; M.I.)

6. All black background
Qly, 1st and 4th, Sable a horse passant argent in chief a crescent for
difference (Percival), 2nd and 3rd, Lockwood, impaling, Qly, 1st and
4th, Argent a canton sable (Sutton), 2nd and 3rd, Barry of four or
and azure a chief qly azure and gules, on the first and fourth two
fleurs-de-lys argent; on the second and third a lion of England (Manners)
Crest: A horse's head couped at the neck proper   Mantling: Gules
and argent   Motto: Resurgam
For Edward Percival (né Lockwood), who m. 1790, Louisa Bridget,
dau. of Lord George Manners-Sutton, and d. 6 July 1804. She d. 5 Feb.
1800.   (Burke's Commoners)

LANGDON HILLS

1. All black background
On a lozenge   Qly of eleven, 1st and 11th, Vert a chevron between
three garbs or (Hatton), 2nd, Argent a cross flory between four martlets
gules (Goleborne), 3rd, Argent an eagle displayed sable armed proper
(Brune), 4th, Gules a fess or between three dolphins naiant vert

(Ascham), 5th, Or a bend between three roundels sable (Cotton), 6th
Or three piles in point gules (Scott), 7th, Or a lion rampant within a
double tressure flory counterflory gules (Stewart), 8th, Argent a
lion rampant azure a chief gules (Waltheof), 9th, Or a lion rampant
gules (David, King of Scots), 10th, Azure six garbs, three, two and
one or (Kevelioc)
On the reverse is a note: Prepared by Charles Roberson, 51 Long
Acre, London
For Susannah, 5th dau. of Sir Thomas Hatton, Bt. She d. unm. 4 Mar.
1842, aged 81.   (M.I.; E.A. II, 1277)
(This hatchment, recorded in 1953, was in an exhibition at Prittlewell
Priory in 1966, but went missing: it has been found and is now in the
church which has become a private residence)

LAWFORD

1. All black background
Sable a saltire argent between four lions' gambs erased or (Nunn)
Crest: A bull's head erased per fess argent and gules   Mantling:
Gules and argent   Motto: Resurgam
Probably for Thomas William Nunn, d. 16 May 1888, aged 56.
(M.I.)

2. Dexter background black
Azure a chevron ermine between three stags statant or, a chief or
(Green)   In pretence: Qly, 1st and 4th, Argent on a bend sable
three lozenges ermine (Dent), 2nd and 3rd, Argent on a bend azure
three cross crosslets fitchy or (   )
No crest   Mantling: Gules and argent   Motto: Expurgiscimine
horam nescitis   Skull below
For Edward Green, who m. Catherine, dau. and heiress of Charles
Dent, and d. 26 Apr. 1778.   (M.I.; E.A., I, 635)

3. Dexter background black
Green   In pretence: Sable a cross ermine between four escallops
argent (Pleasance)
Crest: A stag's head erased or   Mantling: Gules and argent
Motto: Resurgam
For Edward Green, who m. Elizabeth, and d. 16 June 1814, aged 69.
(M.I.)

4. All black background
Azure three wild men in fess proper each holding in his dexter hand a
club and in his sinister a shield argent charged with a cross gules
(Wood)

Crest: A tree proper   Mantling: Gules and argent
Motto: In coelo quies
For the Rev. William Wood, B.D., Rector of Lawford, 1805–1821,
d. 26 Dec. 1821, aged 75.   (M.I.)

LAYER MARNEY

1. Sinister background black
Qly, 1st, Azure a griffin segreant or (Corsellis), 2nd, Or a boar's head
couped in bend sable langued gules (   ), 3rd, Argent three
chevronels azure (   ), 4th, Gules a battleaxe in pale argent (   )
In pretence: Qly, 1st and 4th, Vert two bars engrailed or in fess point
a leopard's face and in chief two leopards' faces or (Child), 2nd and
3rd, Argent a fess between three fleurs-de-lys sable (Evance)
Crest: A demi-griffin or   Mantling: Gules and argent   Motto:
Spes alit
For Frances, dau. of Sir Caesar Child, of Woodford, who m. Nicholas
Corsellis, of Lincolns Inn, and d.   He d. 1761.
(E.A., IV, 280; Berry's Essex Pedigrees, 651)

2. Dexter background black
Qly, 1st and 4th, Azure a griffin segreant or, a crescent for cadency
(Corsellis), 2nd and 3rd, Vert two bars between three leopards' faces
or (Child), impaling, Argent on the sea proper a lymphad sable with
flag and pennon gules, on a chief gules three bezants each charged
with a molet or (Utterson)
Crest and mantling: As 1.   Motto: Non est mortale quod opto
For Matthews Corsellis, of Layer Marney Towers, who m. Louisa, dau.
of John Utterson, of Marwell Hall, Fareham, Hants, and d.s.p. 14
Dec. 1855.   (Sources, as 1; M.I.; M.G. and H. 5th ser. Vol. I)

LITTLE LEIGHS

1. All black background
Qly of six, 1st and 6th, Per fess azure and argent a fess counter-
embattled or, in chief a molet of six points argent, in base on a mount
vert an elm proper (Olmius), 2nd, Argent six bezants, three, two and
one, on a chief sable a deer's head couped azure, over the ears a ducal
coronet or (Reinstein), 3rd, Vert a goat rampant argent (Cappre),
4th, Argent an arm vested proper issuant from a cloud on the sinister
side and holding a sprig of wheat proper (Gerverdiney), 5th, Sable a
herring in bend or (Drigue)

Crest: A demi-Moor in armour proper, garnished or, between two laurel branches vert wreathed argent and gules, on a belt a fess counter-embattled or, on the fess a crescent gules   Mantling: Gules and argent   Motto: In coelo quies
For Herman Olmius, sixth and second surviving son of Herman Olmius of the Warren House, and of Judith Drigue, and d. 24 Apr. 1726, aged 42.   (M.I.; Wright's Essex, II, 18 footnote)

2. Dexter background black
Azure a saltire or between four cinquefoils gules (Wellstead), impaling, Per chevron sable and argent three bells counterchanged (Porter)
Crest: A doe trippant proper   Mantling: Gules and argent
Motto: Bien étayé
For James Wellstead of West Ham, Essex, who m. 1814, Louisa Porter, of Great Waltham, and d. 2 Feb. 1843, aged 49.   (M.I. in churchyard)

MALDON

1. Dexter background black
Argent on a chevron sable between three roses gules stalked and leaved vert three fleurs-de-lys or (Coape), impaling, Or an annulet sable between three crescents gules ( )
Crest: A fleur-de-lys per pale or and argent   Mantling: Gules and argent   Motto: Aequo adeste animo
Probably for Henry Coape, who d. 1848.   (Memorial window; E.A., III, 2459)

2. All black background
On a lozenge   Sable three pickaxes or (Piggott), impaling, Coape
Mantling: Gules and argent   Motto: Resurgam   Cherub's head above
Unidentified   (E.Anglian, II, 139)

3. All black background
Argent on a chevron embattled between three dolphins sable three molets of six points or (Coe)
Crest: A talbot's head erased proper collared argent   Mantling: Gules and argent   Motto: In coelo quies   Skull below
Probably for Charles Coe, d. 2 Aug. 1738, aged 76. His wife Hannah, d. 26 Sept. 1730, aged 58.   (M.I.; E.Anglian II, 139)

MARGARETTING

1. Dexter background black
Vairy argent and sable on a chief or three molets pierced sable
(Benyon), impaling, Argent three piles one in chief between two in
base sable (Hulse)
Crest: A griffin sejant wings displayed argent collared vair langued
gules   Mantling: Gules and argent   Motto: Resurgam
Cherubs' heads in folds of mantling
For Richard Benyon, M.P., who m. 1767, Hannah, eldest dau. of Sir
Edward Hulse, Bt. of Breamore House, and d. 22 Aug. 1796, aged 50.
She d. 27 Apr. 1828.   (B.L.G. 2nd ed.; M.I.)

2. Sinister background black
Vair on a chief or three molets sable (Benyon), impaling, Per pale
nebuly or and azure six martlets counterchanged (Fleetwood)
Motto: Mors janua vitæ
Unidentified   (E. Anglian, II, 105)

3. Dexter background black
Ermine three bendlets azure (Vachell)   In pretence: Sable a lion
rampant between eight cross crosslets argent and a bordure ermine
(Long)
Crest: A bull statant proper collared and belled or   Mantling: Gules
and argent   Motto: Resurgam
For Richard Vachell, of Copfold Hall, who m. 1783, Margaret, dau.
of the Rev. Richard Long, and d. 13 Apr. 1828.
(Alumni Cantabrigienses; M.I. in churchyard)

4. All black background
On a lozenge   Vachell   In pretence: Long
Motto: Resurgam   Cherub's head above
For Margaret, widow of Richard Vachell, d. 21 July, 1833.
(Source, as 3)

MESSING

1. Dexter background black
Sable a fess dancetty between two leopards' faces or, the Badge of
Ulster (Luckyn), impaling, Argent on a fess sable three molets
or and in dexter chief an ermine spot (Grimston)
Crest: Out of a tower chequy or and sable a demi-griffin or
Motto: Moriendo vivo
For Sir Capell Luckyn, 2nd Bt., of Messing Hall, who m. 1648, Mary,
dau. of Sir Harbottle Grimston of Bradfield, and d. 23 Jan, 1679, aged
40.   (B.P. 1949 ed. Verulam; Morant I, 177)

2. All black background
On a lozenge   Arms: As 1.
Motto: In morte quies
For Mary, widow of Sir Capell Luckyn, 2nd Bt. She d. 18 Mar. 1719.
(Source, as 1)

3. Dexter background black
Luckyn, with Badge of Ulster, impaling, Gules two flaunches chequy
argent and azure (Sherington)
Crest: As 1.   Mantling: Gules and argent   Motto: As 1.
For Sir William Luckyn, 3rd Bt., of Messing Hall, who m. Mary, dau. of
William Sherington, Alderman of London, and d. 1708.   (B.P. 1949 ed.)

4. All black background
Luckyn, with Badge of Ulster
Crest: As 1.   Mantling: Gules and argent   Motto: Mors janua vitæ
For Sir Harbottle Luckyn, 4th Bt., who d. unm. 4 Feb. 1736/7.
(B.P. 1949 ed.; M.I. in churchyard)

5. All black background
Gules a chevron argent between three rings or a crescent for difference
(   )   In pretence: Vert a saltire or (Hunt)
Crest: A horse's head erased argent   Mantling: Gules and argent
Motto: Mors janua vitæ
Unidentified   (E.A. IV, 3040)

NAZEING

1. Dexter background black
Argent on two bars sable three trefoils slipped or, in chief a greyhound
courant sable (Palmer), impaling, Argent a chevron between three
horseshoes sable (Fearon)
Crest: A greyhound sejant sable collared and charged on the shoulder
with a trefoil slipped or   Mantling: Gules and argent   Motto:
Resurgam
For Sir Ralph Palmer, sixth and youngest son of William and Mary
Palmer of Nazeing. He m. Margaret Eliza, eldest dau. of Maj.-Gen.
Fearon, C.B., and d. 25 Jan. 1838, aged 54. She d. 15 Mar. 1867.
(B.P. 1959 ed.; M.I.)

2. Dexter background black
Qly, 1st and 4th, Argent on two bars sable three trefoils slipped argent,
in chief a greyhound courant sable (Palmer), 2nd, Azure on a chevron
or between three swans argent three cinquefoils gules (Charlton), 3rd,
Gyronny of eight argent and azure, on a canton gules a fleur-de-lys or

(Pickard)   In pretence: Qly, 1st and 4th, Gules three eagles' legs
erased at the thigh or (Bund), 2nd and 3rd, Azure a chevron ermine
between three trefoils slipped argent (Meade)
Crest: A greyhound sejant sable collared and charged on the
shoulder with a trefoil slipped argent   Mantling: Gules and argent
Motto: Palma virtute
For George Palmer, who m. 1795, Anna Maria, dau. and co-heir of
William Bund of Wick, co. Worcs, and d. 12 May 1853, aged 81.
She d. 13 Oct. 1856.   (B.P. 1959 ed.)

NOAK HILL

1. Dexter background black
Argent on a cross sable five fleurs-de-lys or, in dexter chief the Badge
of Ulster (Neave)   In pretence: Gules two lions passant between
three roses in pale argent barbed azure (Hughes)
Crest: From a ducal coronet or a lily stalked and leaved proper
Mantling: Sable and argent   Motto: Sola proba quae honesta
For Sir Arundell Neave, D.L., 4th Bt., who m. 1871, Gwyn Gertrude,
youngest dau. of William, 1st Baron Dinorben, and d. 21 Sept. 1877.
(B.P. 1949 ed.)
(There is another hatchment for Sir Arundell at Llanwellwyfo,
Anglesey)

NORTH OCKENDON

1. Dexter background black
Qly, 1st and 4th, Argent on a chevron between three cross crosslets
fitchy sable an escallop or (Russell), 2nd, Argent three palmers staves
sable ends or (Palmer), 3rd, Argent on a bend sable three owls argent
(Savile), impaling, Per pale indented or and gules (Bermingham)
Crest: On a demi-lion rampant argent collared gules a chevron sable
charged with an escallop or, the dexter paw holding a cross crosslet
fitchy sable   Mantling: Gules and argent   Motto: Resurgam
For Joseph Russell, who d. 15 Feb. 1828, aged 69.   (M.I.)

2. All black background
On a lozenge surmounted by a cherub's head
Arms: As 1.
Motto: Resurgam
For Elizabeth, widow of Joseph Russell, d. 13 Feb. 1838, aged 86.
(M.I.)

HIGH ONGAR

1. Dexter background black
Qly, 1st and 4th, Argent a bend cotised sable (Stane), 2nd and 3rd, Or on a fess sable three roundels argent (Bramston), impaling, Sable two shinbones in saltire the dexter surmounting the sinister argent (Newton)
Crests: 1. A dexter hand proper grasping a battleaxe pointing to the sinister argent headed or   2. A lion sejant or collared sable, the collar charged with three roundels argent   Mantling: Gules and argent   Motto: In coelo quies
For the Rev. John Bramston-Stane, of Forest Hall, who m. 1801, Mary Elizabeth Newton, of Antigua, and d. 21 Feb. 1857, aged 83. (M.I.)

ORSETT

1. Dexter background black
Qly, 1st and 4th, Or a greyhound courant between two bars sable (Baker), 2nd and 3rd, Gules a chevron argent between three helmets proper (Cholmley), impaling, Azure a fess nebuly between three crescents, between the horns of each an estoile or (Bateman)
Crest: Out of a ducal coronet a cockatrice or   Mantling: Gules and argent   Motto: Mors janua vitæ
For Richard Baker, of Orsett Hall, who m. Elizabeth Bateman, and d. 22 Apr. 1751, aged 43.   (M.I.; E.A., I, 317)

2. All black background
On a lozenge surmounted by a cherub's head
Arms: As 1.
Motto: In coelo quies
For Elizabeth, widow of Richard Baker. She d. 5 Oct. 1790, aged 80. (M.I.; E.A., I, 317)

3. All black background
A shield and a lozenge
Shield   Baker, with crescent for cadency, impaling, Argent on a fess gules cotised sable three pairs of wings conjoined in lure argent (Wingfield)
Lozenge   Ermine on a cross gules five bezants, in centre chief the Badge of Ulster (St Aubyn), impaling, Wingfield
Crest: A cockatrice or   Mantling: Gules and argent   Motto: Resurgam   Cherub's head below
For John Baker, who m. 1782, Elizabeth, dau. of William Wingfield, relict of Sir John St Aubyn, Bt., and d. 1 May 1801, aged 55. She d. 28 July 1796.   (M.I.; E.A., I, 317)

4. Dexter background black
Baker, impaling, Qly, 1st and 4th, Or a griffin segreant gules (Trafford),
2nd and 3rd, Argent three cinquefoils gules (Southwell)
Crest: Out of a ducal coronet a cockatrice or　　　Mantling: Gules and
argent　　　Motto: Resurgam
For Richard Baker, who m. Jane, dau. of Sir Clement Trafford and
Jane Trafford-Southwell, and d. 9 July 1827, aged 82.　　(B.L.G. 5th
ed.; M.I.; E.A., I, 317)

5. All black background
On a lozenge　　　Arms: As 4.
Motto: Resurgam
For Jane, widow of Richard Baker. She d. 19 Feb. 1849, aged 85.
(Sources, as 4.)

6. All black background
On a lozenge surmounted by a cherub's head
Argent a griffin segreant gules holding an escutcheon argent charged
with a wolf's head sable (Trafford)　　　In pretence: Argent three
cinquefoils gules (Southwell)
Motto: Resurgam
For Jane, dau. of Edward Southwell, of Wisbech, who m. Sir Clement
Boehm Trafford, of Dunton Hall, Lincs. She assumed the additional
name of Southwell, and d. 21 Apr. 1809. He d. 1786.
(M.I.; B.L.G. 5th ed.; E.A., I, 317)

7. All black background
On a lozenge surmounted by a cherub's head　　　Or a greyhound
courant between two bars sable (Baker)　　　Skull below
Motto: Resurgam
Unidentified

8. Exactly as last, but without skull below lozenge, and no motto
Unidentified

9. All black background
Argent on a bend gules cotised sable three pairs of wings conjoined in
lure argent (Wingfield)
Crest: A griffin passant or　　　Mantling: Gules and argent
Motto: Resurgam
Probably for William Wingfield, who inherited the estates of the
Manor of Orsett in 1849. He died at Sherborne in 1859.
(Brooks, William Palmer and his school)

10. All black background
Qly, 1st and 4th, Or three shuttles sable (Shuttleworth), 2nd and 3rd,
Or three boars' heads erased sable (Barton)

Crest: An arm vested azure cuffed argent holding a shuttle sable
Mantling: Gules and argent   Motto: Resurgam
Probably for Robert Shuttleworth, of Gawthorp Hall, and Barton
Lodge, Lancs, who d. 29 Jan. 1816, aged 71.   (M.I.; E.A., III,
2744)

11. All black background

Argent on a pile sable three fusils argent (Freeman)
Crest: A demi-lion rampant gules collared fusilly or   Mantling:
Gules and or   Motto: In coelo quies
Probably for John Freeman, of Orsett, who d. 30 Apr. 1747.
(M.I.)

12. Sinister background black

Or three bats displayed sable (Usko), impaling, Argent on a mound
vert a man walking habited in a long russet gown with wide sleeves, his
feet sandalled, head bare and hair dishevelled, holding in the dexter
hand a long cross potent all proper (   )
Motto: Resurgam   Shield surmounted by a lover's knot and two
cherubs' heads
For Henrietta Elizabeth, wife of the Rev. John Frederick Usko, Rector
of Orsett for 33 years. She d. 19 July 1818, aged 41. He d. 31 Dec.
1841, aged 81.   (E.A., IV, 318; East Anglian, 1869, III, 16; M.I.)

13. All black background

A shield and a lozenge   Shield   Vert fretty or (Whitmore)
Crest: A falcon on a stump of a tree with a branch springing from the
dexter proper   Mantling: Gules and argent
Motto: In corrupta fides
Lozenge   Qly, 1st and 4th, Sable a chevron ermine between three
otters argent (Hartopp), 2nd and 3rd, Per saltire argent and gules
crusilly and three boars' heads all counterchanged (Cradock)
For Thomas Charles Douglas Whitmore, J.P., D.L., who m. 1867,
Louisa Margaret Emily, 5th dau. of Sir William Cradock-Hartopp,
3rd Bt., and d. 16 Feb. 1907. She d. 29 Nov. 1892.
(B.L.G. 1937 ed.)

14. All black background (should be S.Bl.)

Whitmore, impaling, Ermine a tree-trunk in bend eradicated proper
between three foxes' heads gules (Houldsworth)
Motto: Incorrupta fides
For Violet Frances Elisabeth, dau. of Sir William Houldsworth, 1st Bt.,
who m. 1900, as his first wife, Colonel Francis Henry Douglas Charlton
Whitmore, and d. 13 June 1927.   (B.L.G. 1937 ed.)
(Hatchment painted by Sir Francis Whitmore)

PAGLESHAM

1. Dexter background black
Per bend azure and gules a bend or (Massu)
Crest: A stork proper
No mantling, but chains of green oak leaves with interlacing gold
medallions   Motto: Resurgam   Winged skull below
For John Massu, of Langtons, Hornchurch and Paglesham, d. 18 Dec.
1807, aged 49.   (E.A., I, 506)

PENTLOW

1. Dexter background black
Azure three lions rampant and on a chief argent three cross crosslets
sable (Mathew)   In pretence: Qly, 1st and 4th, Azure a molet
pierced argent (Coldham), 2nd and 3rd, Argent fretty gules a cross
argent, a bordure sable semy of cinquefoils argent (Brice)
Crest: A lion's gamb erect holding a cross crosslet sable
Mantling: Gules and argent   Motto: Non omnis moriar
For William Mathew, who m. 1787, Elizabeth Maria, dau. of Edward
Coldham, of Bury St Edmunds, and d. 17 June 1830.   (M.I.)

2. All black background
On a lozenge   Mathew   In pretence: Coldham
Mantling: Gules and argent   Motto: Non omnis moriar
For Elizabeth Maria, widow of William Mathew. She d. 17 Feb. 1835,
aged 80.   (M.I.)

3. Dexter background black
Qly, 1st and 4th, Mathew, 2nd, Coldham, 3rd, Brice, impaling, Per
bend argent and sable three trefoils counterchanged (Johnson)
Crests: Dexter, A lion's gamb erect holding a cross crosslet sable
Sinister, A griffin's head erased or the neck pierced with an arrow
proper   Mantling: Gules and argent   Motto: Resurgam
For the Rev. Edward William Mathew, who m. 1815, Charlotte Olivia,
2nd dau. of Oliver Johnson of the Hay House, Earls Colne, and d.
9 Aug. 1834, aged 45.   (M.I.; B.L.G. 7th ed.)

PURLEIGH

1. Dexter background black
Argent a cross gules quarter-pierced nine cross crosslets, three, three
and three counterchanged a canton ermine (Bonnell), impaling, Gules a

chevron and in chief a bar argent (   )
Crest: A demi-lion or spotted sable langued gules, tail forked and
interlaced, in the paws a spear or   Mantling: Gules and argent
Motto: Terris peregrinus et hospes
Probably for James Harvey Bonnell, d. 27 Feb. 1869, aged 40. His wife,
Elizabeth, d. 23 Mar. 1883, aged 77.
(E.R.O. T/Z20/8; M.I. in churchyard)
(Hatchment placed in church by H. Hudson, Lord of the Manor of
Purleigh, in 1936)

RAINHAM

1. All black background
Qly azure and argent in the first and fourth quarters a cross moline
argent (Crosse)
Crest: On a chapeau gules and ermine a stork azure holding in its dexter
claw a cross moline argent   Mantling: Gules and argent
Motto: Toujours pret
For the Rev. H. G. G. Crosse, Vicar of Rainham, d. 17 July 1865,
aged 63.   (Inscription on back of hatchment; parish guide)

RAMSDEN BELLHOUSE

1. All black background
Azure three fleurs-de-lys within a bordure engrailed or (Unwin)
Crest: A fleur-de-lys or   Mantling: Gules and argent
Motto: (worn away; letters BE only remaining)   Winged skull below
For the Rev. William Cawthorn Unwin, Rector 1769–1786, who
d. 30 Nov. 1786.   (E.A., III, 2514; E.Anglian, 1866, II, 304;
Musgrave's Obituary)

RAMSEY

1. Dexter background black
Qly, 1st and 4th, Ermine on a mount vert issuant from park palings
with gate proper a lion rampant or holding in the sinister paw five
arrows sable and in the dexter paw a scimitar argent, pommel and hilt
or, on a chief indented sable two lions rampant argent langued gules
(Burr), 2nd and 3rd, Gules a lion rampant ermine holding in his
paws a ducal coronet or between eight fleurs-de-lys argent
(Davall)   In pretence: Qly of six, 1st, Gules on a bend ermine a lion

passant sable in sinister chief a rose argent (Davis), 2nd, Vert on a
chevron between three stags' heads cabossed or three molets sable
(Higford), 3rd, Per pale argent and gules on a bend three escallops all
counterchanged (   ), 4th, Argent a pile sable (   ), 5th, Gules a
bend between six pears stalks downwards or (   ), 6th, Gules
three stirrups two and one leathered or (Scudamore)
Crest: Out of a mural crown argent inscribed with the word 'Ternate'
a Malay holding in the dexter hand the colours of Ternate, all proper
Mantling: Gules and argent   Motto: Virtus verus honos
From the dexter side of shield issuant a battle axe and two flags, one
vert the other or, and from the sinister side, a sword proper with two
flags, one or the other vert
For Lt.-Gen. Daniel Burr, who m. 1808, as his 2nd wife, Mary, dau.
and co-heir of James Davis of Chepstow, Mon., and d. 19 Feb. 1828,
aged 78.
(B.L.G. 5th ed.; M.I.; E.A., IV, 2932)

RIVENHALL

1. Sinister background black
Sable a chevron between in chief two crescents and in base a trefoil
slipped or (Western), impaling, Argent a bend between two lions
rampant sable langued gules (Osborne)   Cherub's head above shield
For Mary, dau. of Admiral Henry Osborne, who m. the Rev. Thomas
Walsingham Western, and d. 7 June 1823, aged 76.
(Essex Review, 1901, X, 1)

2. All black background
Arms: As 1.
Crest: A demi-lion in the dexter paw a trefoil slipped or
No helm or mantling   Motto: Nec temere nec timide
For the Rev. Thomas Walsingham Western, who d. 2 Sept. 1823,
aged 75.   (Source, as 1.)

3. All black background
Qly, 1st and 4th, Western, 2nd and 3rd, Paly of six or and azure a
canton ermine (Shirley)
Baron's coronet   Crest: A demi-lion rampant or langued gules holding
in the dexter paw a trefoil slipped vert   No mantling   Supporters:
Dexter, A lion or langued gules gorged with a collar azure pendant
therefrom an escutcheon charged with the arms of Western
Sinister, A stag gules attired argent gorged with a ducal coronet or,
pendant therefrom an escutcheon charged with the arms of Shirley

Motto: As 2.
For Charles, Baron Western, who d. unm. 13 Nov. 1844, aged 77.
(M.I.)

4. All black background
Gules out of each of three mural crowns argent a demi-lion rampant
or langued azure (   )
Crest: Out of a mural crown or a demi-lion rampant argent holding
between the paws a block proper
No mantling   Motto: Mors janua vitæ   To dexter a palm branch
and to sinister an olive branch   Winged skull in base
Unidentified

ROYDON

1. Dexter background black
Azure a bend between six covered cups or (Butler), impaling, Or three
lions passant in pale sable langued gules (Carew)
Crest: From a ducal coronet a dexter hand grasping a covered cup or
Mantling: Gules and argent   Motto: In morte quies
For Francis Butler, who m. as his 2nd wife, Elizabeth, dau. of Henry
Carew, of Stonecastle, Kent, and d. 4 Aug. 1721, aged 76.   (M.I.)

2. All black background
Argent three palmers' staves sable garnished or (Palmer), impaling,
Argent on a bend sable three eagles displayed or (Ernle)
Crest: A dexter cubit arm cuffed and vambraced proper holding a
palmer's staff sable garnished or   Mantling: Gules and argent
Motto: His saladinum vicimus armis
For Ralph Palmer, who m. Catherine, only child of Sir John Ernle,
and d. 1744/5, will proved Mar. 1745.   (Gen. Mag. 1926)

3. Dexter background black
Qly, 1st, Palmer, 2nd, Gules a fess between in chief a stag courant and
in base three molets of six points or (Hamey), 3rd, Argent a fess sable
between in chief a demi-lion issuant gules and in base three molets
of six points in fess sable (Oeils), 4th, Per pale or and gules a pair of
wings conjoined in lure counterchanged, a chief sable (   ),
impaling, Gules on a fess engrailed or between three bezants each
charged with a peacock's head erased azure three mascles sable
(Peacock)
Crest and mantling: As 2.   Motto: Mors janua vitæ   Winged
skull below
For Ralph Palmer, who m. Elizabeth Peacock, and d. 23 Jan. 1755.
(Gen. Mag. 1926)

4. All black background
Qly, 1st and 6th, Sable a lion rampant between six cross crosslets
argent (Long), 2nd, Argent a chevron between three griffins' heads
erased gules (Tylney), 3rd, Gules a chevron ermine between three
eagles close argent (Child), 4th, qly i. & iv. Argent a double-headed
eagle displayed sable, ii. & iii. Argent three firebrands sable flammant
proper, over all on an escutcheon argent a man's leg couped at the
thigh sable (Glynne), 5th, Argent on a bend azure three escallops
argent (Bernard)   In fess point the Badge of Ulster
Crest: From a ducal coronet or a demi-lion rampant argent langued
gules   Mantling: Gules and argent   Motto: Mors janua vitæ
For Sir James Tylney-Long, 8th and last Bt., who d. 14 Sept. 1805,
aged 11.   (B.E.B.; E.A., I, 236; E. Anglian, 1869, IV, 17)

5. Dexter background black
Argent three boars' heads erased and erect proper (Booth), impaling,
Argent on a chevron azure between three trefoils slipped sable
three crescents or (Williamson)
Crest: A lion passant argent langued gules   Mantling: Gules and
argent   Motto: Deus adjuvat nos
For William Booth, of Roydon House, who m. Mary, dau. and co-heir
of John Williamson, and d. 17 Oct. 1834.   (B.P. 1875 ed.)
(There is another hatchment for William Booth at Stanstead Abbots,
Herts)

6. All black background
On a lozenge   Argent three boars' heads erased and erect proper, a
crescent for difference (Booth)   In pretence: Williamson
For Elizabeth, dau. and co-heir of John Williamson, who m. John
Gillyat Booth, and d.   (B.P. 1875 ed.)
(There is another hatchment for Elizabeth Booth at Stanstead Abbots,
Herts)

LITTLE SAMPFORD

1. Dexter background black
Two oval shields   Dexter, within the Order of Hanover, Qly, 1st
and 4th, Or a saltire gules a molet for difference (Eustace), 2nd, Barry
of six or and azure (FitzEustace), 3rd, Argent two bars nebuly
sable (   )   Sinister, Qly as dexter, with in pretence, Or on a
chief indented sable three crescents argent (Harvey)
Crest: A stag statant proper   Mantling: Gules and argent
Motto: Cur me persequeris   Crosses of Orders of Hanover and
Bath pendent below shield

For Lieut.-Gen. Sir William Cornwallis Eustace, K.C.H., C.B., of
Sampford Hall, who m. 3rd, Emma, 2nd dau. and co-heir of Admiral
Sir Eliab Harvey, and d. 9 Feb. 1855.　　　(B.E.P.; B.L.G. 5th ed.)

2. All black background
Oval shield and lozenge.　　　Arms: As 1.
Orders pendent below shield, as 1.
For Emma, widow of Gen. Sir William Cornwallis Eustace. She d. 9
Mar. 1865, aged 77.　　　(M.I. in churchyard)

SANDON

1. Dexter background black
Per chevron engrailed or and azure three martlets counterchanged ·
(Hodgson), impaling, Argent a chevron between three lions' heads
erased gules crowned or (Buckel)
Crest: A dove, in its beak an olive branch proper　　　Mantling: Gules
and argent　　　Motto: Pace in bello
Unidentified　　　(Bloom, E.R.O. T/P72/1)

2. Dexter background black
Gules a pelican in her piety on her nest or (Carne), impaling, Azure
a lion rampant or armed and langued gules (　　　)
Crest: A griffin's head erased gules　　　Mantling: Gules and argent
Motto: Resurgam
For Frederick Carne Rasch, who d. 22 Feb. 1876, aged 67.
(M.I.; E.A., I, 181, 2 and 3)

3. All black background
On a lozenge surmounted by a cherub's head
Arms: As 2.
Motto: Resurgam
For Catherine, widow of Frederick Carne Rasch. She d. 9 April 1881,
aged 70.　　　(M.I.; Bloom, E.R.O. T/P72/1)

SHENFIELD

1. All black background
Qly, 1st, Or a lion rampant gules (Vaughan), 2nd, Per fess sable and
argent a lion rampant counterchanged (Vaughan), 3rd, Argent a fess
engrailed sable between three apples slipped vert (Appleton), 4th,
Gules on a bend between two lions passant argent three partridges
sable (Partridge)

Crest: From a ducal coronet or a lion rampant gules
Mantling: Gules and argent   Mottoes: (above) Fide et amore
(below) In coelo quies   Skull below
Probably for Richard Vaughan, d. 17 Oct. 1780.
(E.A., I, 210; King, Insignia gentilitia; E.R.O., T/8196)

2. Dexter background black
Per pale argent and sable a chevron between three talbots passant
counterchanged, on a chief gules three leopards' faces or (Gooch)
In pretence: Per chevron or and sable a lion rampant counterchanged,
on a canton sable a fleur-de-lys or (Barker)
Crest: A talbot counterchanged (with background of hatchment)
Mantling: Gules and argent   Motto: Fide et virtute
Unidentified

3. Dexter background black
Argent on a chevron sable between three dolphins embowed proper
three towers argent (Gillum), impaling, Or four bars sable (   )
Crest: A dolphin embowed proper   Mantling: Gules and argent
Motto: Mors janua vitæ
Probably for Stephen Fryer Gillum, of Middleton Hall, who d. Oct.
1826, aged 57. His widow d. July 1827, aged 41.   (Par. Regs.)

STANFORD-LE-HOPE

1. Dexter background black
Gules two chevronels or between three swans' wings elevated argent
(Scratton), impaling, Argent on a chevron azure between three demi-
unicorns courant gules three acorn slips or (Colliar)
Crest: A wolf's head erased proper, in the mouth a trefoil slipped
proper   Mantling: Gules and argent   Motto: In Deo fides
For John Scratton, who d. 26 Apr. 1841, aged 53. His wife,
Elizabeth, d. 23 June 1864, aged 78.   (M.I.)

2. Dexter background black
Scratton, impaling, Azure three fishes naiant in pale argent (Kersteman)
Crest and mantling: As 1.   Motto: Resurgam
For James Scratton, who m. Judith, dau. of Jeremiah Kersteman, of
Canewdon (q.v.), and d. 16 Apr. 1837, aged 86. She d. 18 Oct. 1838,
aged 87.   (M.I.; E.R.O., D/DQS/186)

STAPLEFORD TAWNEY

1. Sinister background black
Qly, 1st, Argent a saltire azure between three crescents and in base a

dolphin embowed sable (Smith), 2nd, Argent a ship in a storm at sea proper (Smith), 3rd, Azure a wild cat sejant guardant argent (Smith), 4th, Or a crescent gules (Smith), impaling, Sable a leg couped at the thigh in armour proper garnished and spurred or between two spears palewise points upwards or (Gilbert)
No crest or helm, but above shield a human face, from which issues laterally a mantle gules and argent   Motto: Marte et ingenio
Inscribed on frame 'Hatchment of Joshua Smith, Esq., M.P. for Devises of Erl Stoke Pk, Wilts.'
Despite inscription on frame almost certainly for the wife of Joshua Smith

STEBBING

1. Dexter background black
Sable a fess ermine between three dexter hands couped argent (Batt)
In pretence: Sable three crescents argent (   )
. Crest: A demi-lion rampant or gutty gules in the dexter paw a baton sable tipped or   Mantling: Gules and argent   Motto: Mors janua vitæ
For Arthur Batt, who d. 3 Feb. 1730, aged 47.   (M.I.)

2. All black background
On a lozenge   Arms: As 1.
For Frances, widow of Arthur Batt. She d. 23 Feb. 1744.   (M.I.)

STEEPLE BUMPSTEAD

1. Dexter background black
Per pale gules and azure a fess indented argent gutty gules between three hawks or (Stephens)
Crest: A lion rampant argent spotted gules   Mantling: Gules and argent   Motto: Resurgam
Possibly for John Stephens, who m. Frances Elizabeth, dau. of the Rt. Rev. Anthony Ellys, D.D., Bishop of St Davids, and d. 9 Oct. 1799, aged 66.   (M.I.)

2. All black background
On a lozenge   Stephens (hawks proper)   In pretence: Argent a mermaid holding in her dexter hand a glass and in the sinister a comb proper (Ellis)
Mantling and motto: As 3.
For Frances Elizabeth, widow of John Stephens. She d. 24 June 1814, aged 81.   (M.I.)

3. Dexter background black
Qly, 1st and 4th, Stephens, as 2, 2nd and 3rd, Argent a chevron
between three cross crosslets sable (   ), impaling, Paly of six or
and gules, on a bend sable three molets argent (Elton)
Crest: A lion rampant or   Mantling: Gules and argent
Motto: Resurgam
For Ellys Anderson Stephens, who d. 12 Feb. 1845, aged 79. His wife,
Mary, d. 2 July 1847, aged 74. (M.I.)

4. All black background
Qly, 1st and 4th, Ermine on a chief indented sable two eagles
displayed or (Gent), 2nd and 3rd, Or a cross engrailed sable a label
of three points gules each point charged with three bezants (Moyne)
In pretence: Argent a fess and in chief a lion passant gules (Walford)
Crest: Out of a ducal coronet argent a demi-eagle displayed sable
ermined or   Mantling: Gules and argent   Motto: In coelo quies
For George Gent, Esq., of Moyns, who m. Mary, dau. and heiress of
Thomas Walford, of Hersted Hall, Essex, and d. 6 Oct. 1818, aged 94.
She d. 17 Nov. 1802, aged 81.   (B.L.G. 5th ed.; M.I.)

5. All black background
Qly, 1st and 4th, Gent, 2nd and 3rd, Moyne, with one bezant on each
label point, impaling, Argent a cross engrailed gules (Gurney)
Crest: Out of a ducal coronet or a demi-eagle displayed ermine
Mantling: Azure and argent   Motto: Resurgam
Possibly for George William Gent, who d. 17 Mar. 1855, aged 73.
His wife, Eliza Mary, d. 18 Jan. 1846.   (M.I.)

STRETHALL

1. All black background
Sable a chevron between three eagles displayed argent, on a chief
argent a bend engrailed between two martlets sable, in dexter chief a
crescent for difference (Raymond)   In pretence: Azure three
bears' heads couped argent muzzled gules (Forbes)
Crest: A dragon's head erased proper ducally gorged or
Mantling: Gules and argent   Motto: In coelo quies
Probably for the father of the Rev. William Forbes Raymond, Rector,
1820–1856.   (E.A. II, 1455)

SUTTON

1. All black background
Sable a martlet or between three quatrefoils argent, on a chief argent
three garbs sable (White)

Crest: A griffin's head erased sable   Mantling: Gules and argent
Motto: Resurgam   Winged skull below
For John White, native of Rochford, late of this parish, d. 1 Jan. 1792,
aged 93.   (M.I.)

2. Dexter background black
Argent crusilly gules three talbots' heads erased sable (Hall), impaling,
Argent on a bend azure three lovers' knots or (Nott)
Crest: A talbot's head erased sable   Mantling: Gules and argent
Motto: Vixi non sine gloria
Unidentified   (E. Anglian, II, 40)

TERLING

1. Dexter background black
Azure on a chevron argent between three cross crosslets fitchy or
three leopards' faces proper (Strutt)
Baron's coronet   Crest: A demi-lion azure gorged with a mural
coronet or, holding in the dexter paw a cross crosslet fitchy or and
resting the sinister on a shield sable charged with a chevron argent
between three cross crosslets fitchy or   Supporters: Dexter, A
reindeer or collared sable   Sinister, A monkey proper banded
about the middle and chained or
For John James, 2nd Baron Rayleigh, who m. 1842, Clara Elizabeth
La Touche, dau. of Capt. Richard Vicars, R.E., and d. 14 June 1873.
(B.P. 1949 ed.)

THAXTED

1. All black background
Argent a chevron azure between three sinister hands couped gules
(Maynard), impaling, Argent a chevron sable charged with five gouttes
or between three rabbits' heads couped sable each charged with a
goutte or (Rabett)
Viscount's coronet   Crest: A stag proper   Motto: Manus justa
nardus   Supporters: Dexter, A stag proper attired or
Sinister, A talbot argent pied sable collared gules   Winged skull in base
For Henry, 3rd Viscount Maynard, Lord Lieutenant and Vice-Admiral
of Essex, who m. 1810, Mary, dau. of Reginald Rabett, of Bramfield
Hall, and d. 19 May 1865.   (B.P. 1868 ed.)

THEYDON BOIS

1. Dexter background black
Qly, 1st and 4th, Per saltire sable and ermine a lion rampant or
(Grafton), 2nd and 3rd, Argent a lion rampant azure langued gules in
chief two crescents gules (Dare)   In pretence: Gules a bend
cotised wavy argent (Eaton)
Crests: 1. On a barrel an eagle rising in its dexter claw a spear or
2. On a chapeau gules and ermine a demi-lion rampant azure holding
in the paws an increscent gules   Mantling: Gules and argent
Motto: Vivit post funera virtus
For John Marmaduke Grafton-Dare (who took the additional name
of Dare in 1805), who m. 1791, Elizabeth, relict of John Dare of
Bantry Heath, and dau. and co-heir of Henry Eaton, of North
Lodge, Essex, and d. 22 Nov. 1810.   (B.L.G. 7th ed.; M.I.)

2. All black background
On a lozenge   Qly, 1st and 4th, Azure a lion rampant argent
langued gules between three lozenges or each charged with an
increscent gules (Dare), 2nd and 3rd, Qly ermine and sable ermined or
a lion rampant between two cinquefoils in pale or (Grafton)
In pretence: Eaton   Motto: Resurgam   Cherub's head above
For Elizabeth, widow of John Marmaduke Grafton-Dare. She d. 24
Mar. 1823.   (B.L.G. 7th ed.)

3. Dexter background black
Sable on a chevron engrailed between three battleaxes or three eagles
displayed sable (Hall), impaling, Or a lion rampant couped in all the
joints within a double tressure flory counterflory gules (Maitland)
Crest: A horse's head proper semy of molets or, wearing armour and
a plume of two feathers one sable one argent, and carrying in the
mouth a battleaxe or   Mantling: Azure and or   Motto:
Requiescat in pace
Unidentified

4. Dexter background black
Qly, 1st and 4th, Azure a lion rampant argent between three lozenges
or each charged with an increscent gules in chief a cross crosslet or
(Dare), 2nd and 3rd, Hall   In pretence: Qly of six, 1st, qly i. & iv.
Azure a lion rampant argent between three lozenges or each charged
with an increscent gules (Dare), ii. & iii. Per saltire indented ermine
and sable ermined or a lion rampant between two cinquefoils in pale
or (Grafton), 2nd, Per pale gules and azure a bend cotised wavy or
(Eaton), 3rd, Argent three lions rampant azure a crescent for
difference (Mildmay), 4th, Gules on a bend argent three trefoils
slipped vert (Harvey), 5th, Argent a chevron between three eagles'
heads erased azure a crescent for difference (Honywood),

6th, Gules a chevron between three crosses formy fitchy argent
(Bonham)
Crests: 1. A demi-lion rampant azure bezanty charged on the shoulder
with a cross crosslet or, holding between the paws a lozenge or
charged with an increscent gules (Dare)   2. A horse's head in
armour bearing a plume of two feathers one sable one argent holding
in the mouth a battleaxe or (Hall)
Mantling: Azure and argent   Motto: Loyauté sans tache
For Robert Westley Hall-Dare, of Wyefield and Cranbrook, High
Sheriff, Essex, 1821, m. 1815, Elizabeth Grafton, only dau. of John
Marmaduke Grafton-Dare, and d. 20 May 1836.
(B.L.G. 7th ed.; E.A., I, 344a)

5. Dexter background black
Azure a fess nebuly between three crescents ermine (Wild), impaling,
Azure a lion rampant between three fleurs-de-lys or a chief vair
(Hardisty)
Crest: A wyvern sable gutty or collared and chained or
Mantling: Gules and or   Motto: Honor virtutis praemium
For Samuel Wild, who d. 7 Dec. 1807, aged 65.
(M.I.; E.A. III, 2323)

6. All black background
On a lozenge extending to edge of frame
Arms: As 5.
Cherub's head above
For Elizabeth Wild, widow of Samuel Wild, d. 23 Oct. 1844, aged 88.
(Sources, as 5.)

THEYDON GARNON

1. All black background
Azure a chevron between three pheons argent, a crescent on the
chevron for difference (Egerton), impaling, Argent on a bend gules
three leopards' faces or (   )
Crest: A stag's head erased proper   Mantling: Gules, argent, azure
and or   Motto: Resurgam   Winged skull below
For the Rev. Charles Egerton, Vicar of Thorncombe, Devon, and of
Kendal Lodge, who d. 23 Apr. 1845, aged 80. His wife, Mary, d. 7
Dec. 1832, aged 76.   (M.I.)

2. Dexter background black
Argent on a chevron engrailed azure between three trefoils slipped
vert three lozenges or, on a chief azure two arms vested or, issuing from
clouds proper, holding a rose gules barbed vert (Moody), impaling,

Per chevron or and azure three escallops counterchanged (Brinsley)
Crest: Two crossed cubit arms, the dexter vested vert, the sinister
gules, each holding a scimitar argent hilted or   Mantling: Gules and
argent
Motto: In coelo quies   Two cherubs' heads above and a skull below
Probably for Charles Moody, who d. 29 Sept. 1799, aged 45.
(M.I.)

3. All black background
Vert three boars' heads erased or (   ), impaling, Sable a fret argent
(Harington)
Crest: A boar's head erased or   Mantling: Gules and argent
Motto: Resurgam   Winged skull below
Unidentified

4. All black background
On a lozenge   Or two chevronels between three trefoils slipped .
sable (Abdy), impaling, Paly of six azure and ermine, on a chief gules
a lion passant guardant or (Altham)
Motto: In coelo quies
For Harriet, dau. of Peyton Altham, of Markhall, who m. as his 2nd
wife, the Rev. Stotherd Abdy, Rector of Theydon Garnon, and
d. 23 Feb. 1792, aged 63.He d. 3 Apr. 1773.   (B.P. 1939 ed.;M.I.)

5. All black background
Qly, 1st and 4th, Ermine a cross azure (Archer), 2nd and 3rd, Argent
on a chevron azure three cinquefoils or (Eyre)
Crest: A leg in armour couped at the thigh proper   Mantling: Gules
and argent   Motto: In coelo quies   Winged skull below
For William Eyre, who took the name of Archer under the will of
John Archer. He m. Susannah, dau. of Sir John Newton, Bt., and
d. 3 June 1739.   (M.I.)
(All these five hatchments have been restored by Mr. Z. Butrym)

THEYDON MOUNT

1. Sinister background black
Sable a fess dancetty argent billetty sable between three lions
rampant guardant argent each supporting an altar or flaming proper,
in fess point the Badge of Ulster (Smyth), impaling, Azure three swans'
heads erased proper (Hedges)
Motto: Mors janua vitæ   Winged skull above and cherub's head below
For Anne, dau. of the Rt. Hon. Sir Charles Hedges, who m. as his 1st
wife, Sir Edward Smyth, 3rd Bt., and d. 18 Oct. 1719.
(B.P. 1939 ed.)

2. All black background

Qly, 1st and 4th, Smyth, 2nd and 3rd, Argent on a bend sable three
cross crosslets argent in sinister chief a martlet azure (Charnocke),
over all the Badge of Ulster   To dexter of main shield, Smyth,
impaling, Hedges   A.Bl.   To sinister of main shield, Smyth,
impaling, Argent a chevron between three owls gules (Wood) D.Bl.
Crest: A salamander in flames reguardant proper   Mantling: Gules
and argent   Motto: Qua pote lucet   Skull below
For Sir Edward Smyth, 3rd Bt., who m. 1st, Anne, dau. of the Rt.
Hon. Sir Charles Hedges, and 2nd, Elizabeth, dau. of John Wood, of
London, and d. 16 Aug. 1744.   (B.P. 1939 ed.)

3. All black background

On a lozenge surmounted by a cherub's head
Smyth, impaling, Wood
For Elizabeth, 2nd wife of Sir Edward Smyth, 3rd Bt. She d. 23 May,
1748.   (B.P. 1939 ed.)

4. Dexter background black

Qly, 1st and 4th, Smyth, with lions or, 2nd and 3rd, Charnocke, over
all the Badge of Ulster, impaling, Argent a fess chequy or and sable
in chief three cross crosslets fitchy sable (Burgess)
Crest: A salamander in flames reguardant proper ducally gorged or
Mantling: Gules and argent   Motto: Qua pote lucet
For Sir Charles Smyth, 5th Bt., High Sheriff of Essex, 1761, who m.
1760, Elizabeth, dau. of John Burgess of London, and d. 24 Mar. 1773.
She d. 2 Feb. 1776.   (B.P. 1939 ed.)

5. Dexter background black

Qly, 1st and 4th, Smyth, 2nd and 3rd, Charnocke, in centre chief the
Badge of Ulster   In pretence: Gules three demi-woodmen each holding
in the dexter hand over the dexter shoulder a club proper (Wood)
Crest and mantling: As 2.   Cherubs' heads above and skull below
For Sir William Smyth, 6th Bt., who m. Abigail, dau. of Andrew
Wood, of Shrewsbury, and d. 25 Jan. 1777.   (B.P. 1939·ed.)

6. All black background

On a lozenge   Arms: As 5, with Badge of Ulster
Cherub's head above and skull below
For Abigail, widow of Sir William Smyth, 6th Bt. She d. 28 Feb.
1787.   (B.P. 1939 ed.)

7. Sinister background black

Qly, 1st and 4th, Smyth, 2nd and 3rd, Charnocke, in the 1st quarter
the Badge of Ulster   In pretence: Azure a chevron between three
lions' heads erased or (Windham)
Motto: Qua pote lucet

For Anne, only dau. and heiress of John Windham Bowyer, of Waghen,
York, who m. 1779, Sir William Smijth, 7th Bt., and d. 20 Dec. 1815.
(B.P. 1949 ed.)

8. All black background
Arms: As 6, with Badge of Ulster in centre chief
Crests: 1. An eagle rising wings addorsed and inverted sable, holding in
the dexter claw a burning quill proper   2. A salamander in flames
reguardant proper ducally gorged or   Mantling: Gules and argent
Motto: Resurgam
For Sir William Smijth, 7th Bt., who d. 1 May 1823.   (B.P. 1949 ed.)

9. All black background
Qly, 1st and 4th, qly i. & iv. Smyth, ii. & iii. Windham, 2nd and 3rd,
Charnocke   In centre chief the Badge of Ulster
Crests, mantling and motto: As 8.
For Sir Thomas Smijth, 8th Bt., who d. unm. 5 Oct. 1833; or for Sir
John Smijth, 9th Bt., who d. unm. 9 Dec. 1838.   (B.P. 1949 ed.)
(There is an identical hatchment at Horham Hall)

TILTY

1. All black background
Argent a chevron azure between three sinister hands couped at the
wrist gules (Maynard)
Viscount's coronet   Crest: A stag statant or   Mantle: Gules and
ermine   Motto: Manus justa nardus   Supporters: Dexter, A stag
proper attired or   Sinister, A talbot argent pied sable collared gules
For Charles, 1st Viscount Maynard, who d. unm. 30 June 1775, or for
Charles, 2nd Viscount Maynard, who m. Mrs. Anne Horton, and d.s.p.
10 Mar. 1824.   (B.E.P.)

WALTHAM ABBEY

1. All black background
Qly, 1st and 4th, Barry of six argent and azure on each bar argent three
molets gules (Jessopp), 2nd and 3rd, Or a fess between three hinds'
heads erased sable collared or (   )   In pretence: Per bend sable
and or a lion rampant counterchanged (   )
Crest: A dove argent standing on a mound, a spray of leaves issuant to
the dexter proper   Motto: Resurgam   Two cherubs' heads at
top corners of shield
Unidentified

2. Sinister background black
Qly, 1st and 4th, Jessop, 2nd and 3rd, Or three hinds' heads erased
sable (   ), impaling, Argent three bars wavy gules (Drummond)
Motto: In coelo quies   Two cherubs' heads at top corners of shield
Probably for Euphemia Frances, wife of Joseph Jessopp, d. 17 July
1832.   (M.I.)

3. All black background
Arms: As 2.
Crest: As 1.   Motto: Praemia virtutis honores
Probably for Joseph Jessopp, d. 12 Dec. 1859.   (M.I.)

4. Dexter background black
Gules three estoiles of eight points or a canton ermine (Leverton),
impaling, Sable three escallops argent (Strickland)
Crest: A pelican in her piety proper   Mantling: Gules and argent
Motto: Resurgam
For Thomas Leverton, who m. 2nd, Rebecca Strickland, and d. 23
Sept. 1824, aged 81. She d. 4 Aug. 1833, aged 76.   (M.I.s)

5. Dexter background black
Gules a chevron between three cross crosslets fitchy or (Austin),
impaling, Sable in chief two cinquefoils argent in base an escallop or
(? Livingstone)
Crest: A demi-lion rampant proper in the dexter paw a cross crosslet
fitchy or   Mantling: Gules and argent   Motto: Resurgam
Probably for James Austin, who d. 4 June 1803, aged 50. His wife,
Henrietta, d. 4 July 1815, aged 60.   (M.I.)

6. Dexter background black
Qly, 1st and 4th, Or two bars and in chief three roundels gules (Wake),
2nd and 3rd, Argent on a chief vert a cross tau between two pierced
molets or (Drury)   In centre chief the Badge of Ulster
In pretence: Argent a cross between four fleurs-de-lys sable (Fenton)
Crest: A Wake knot or   Mantling: Gules and argent   Motto:
Resurgam   Cherubs' heads flanking shield and winged skull in base
For Sir William Wake, 8th Bt., who m. 1765, Mary (d. 10 Dec. 1823)
only dau. and heiress of William Fenton, and d. 29 Oct. 1785.
(B.P. 1949 ed.)
(Hatchment of widow is in the parish church at Courteenhall,
Northants)

GREAT WALTHAM, Langleys

1. Dexter background black
Azure on a fess between three ostrich feathers argent three martlets

sable (Tufnell), impaling, Qly indented, 1st and 4th, Or four pallets
gules, 2nd and 3rd, Azure a fess couped or between three crescents
argent (des Barres)
Crest: A dexter arm in armour embowed sable, beribboned azure,
holding in the gauntlet a cutlass argent hilted or embrued gules
Mantling: Azure and argent   Motto: Manus haec inimica tyrannis
Painted on plywood
For Nevill Charles Arthur de Hirzel Tufnell, of Langleys, D.L., J.P.,
who m. Josephine Isabella Louise, dau. of Major Joseph des Barres, of
Fermoy, and d. 30 Dec. 1935, aged 71. She d. 14 Sept. 1965, aged 96.
(B.L.G. 18th ed.)

GREAT WALTHAM

1. Dexter background black
Azure on a fess between three ostrich feathers argent three martlets
sable (Tufnell), impaling, Paly of six argent and azure (   )
Crest: A dexter arm in armour proper holding in the gauntlet a cutlass
argent hilted or   Mantling: Gules and argent   Motto: Resurgam
For John Tufnell, d. 3 June 1829. His wife, Hannah, d. 30 Aug. 1836.
(E.R.O., D/DTu 223)

2. All black background
Qly, 1st, Tufnell, 2nd, Sable a cross moline argent (Humphries), 3rd,
Argent on a pile azure three dexter hands couped at the wrist argent
(Jolliffe), 4th, Argent on a canton sable a lion's gamb erased or
(Boothby), impaling, Argent three chevronels gules (Meeke)
Crest: A dexter arm in armour proper elbowed or beribboned gules
holding in the gauntlet a cutlass argent hilted or   Mantling: Gules
and argent   Motto: In coelo quies
For John Jolliffe Tufnell, of Langleys, who m. Anna, dau. of William
Meeke, of Beverley, Yorks, and d. 23 Sept. 1794.
(B.L.G. 1937 ed.; E.A., III, 2427)

3. All black background
Tufnell arms only
Crest: A dexter arm in proper elbowed or holding in the gauntlet
a cutlass argent hilted or   Mantling and motto: As 2.
Probably for Samuel Jolliffe Tufnell, of Langleys, who d. unm. 9 May
1820.   (M.I.; B.L.G. 1937 ed.)

4. All black background
Tufnell arms only
Crest: As 3, but cutlass embrued gules   Mantling: Gules and argent
Motto: Esse quam videre
For Richard Tufnell, of Wallops, Gt. Waltham, d. unm. 1826.
(M.I.; E.A., III, 2427)

5. All black background
On a lozenge Qly, as 2, impaling, Argent a chevron gules between
three garbs azure (Close)
For Anna, eldest dau. of John Close of Easby House, Yorks, who
m. William, 2nd son of John Jolliffe Tufnell, and d. 1824.
(B.L.G. 1937 ed.; ped. in E.R.O., D/DTu 223)

6. All black background
Tufnell, impaling, Argent a cross patonce voided gules
(Pilkington)
Crest: As 3. Mantling: Gules and argent Motto: Resurgam
For John Jolliffe Tufnell, of Langleys, who m. 1801, Catherine
Dorothy, eldest dau. of Sir Michael Pilkington, 6th Bt., and d. 18
July 1864. (B.L.G. 1937 ed.)

(All these hatchments were restored by Mr. and Mrs. K. R. Mabbitt)

WALTON-LE-SOKEN

1. All black background
On a lozenge surmounted by a skull
Qly, 1st and 4th, Per chevron or and sable in chief two fleurs-de-lys
gules and in base five lozenges fesswise or each charged with an
escallop gules (Edgar), 2nd and 3rd, Gules a chevron between three
leopards' faces argent (Edgar)
Mantling: Gules and argent Motto: Fear God A small hatchment
For Katherine, younger dau. of Robert and Elizabeth Edgar, who d.
29 Apr. 1810, aged 70. (per K. Williams)

WETHERSFIELD

1. Dexter background black
Gules an eagle displayed or, on a chief ermine a rose gules between two
martlets sable (Atkinson), impaling, Sable a fess between three
fleurs-de-lys or (Leicester)
Crest: A griffin's head or Mantling: Gules and argent Motto:
Mortal shall put on immortality
For the Rev. Christopher Atkinson, vicar of Wethersfield, who m.
Catherine, dau. of Sir Peter Byrne Leicester, Bt., and d. 18 Mar. 1795.
(B.P. 1875 ed.; E.A., note no 875).

WRITTLE

1. All black background

Argent three bendlets sable each charged with three escallops argent
(Penrose), impaling, Azure on a fess argent between three boars passant
proper three eagles close sable (Bunce)
Crest: A trout naiant or   Mantling: Gules and argent   Motto:
Resurgam
For the Rev. Thomas Penrose, who d. 1851.   (Church guide)
(Destroyed by fire in 1974)

HERTFORDSHIRE

by

A. W. Longden

Wheathampstead: For Anne Drake-Garrard, 1827
(Photograph by Mr. D.R. Pratt)

INTRODUCTION

Of the 93 hatchments recorded most are in good condition; several churches have had their hatchments cleaned, repaired and rehung, which is a very encouraging sign. A few have disappeared during the past few years usually after the redecoration of the church, when it was probably thought that they looked too damaged to repair. At Hemel Hempstead one behind the organ to a Lord Polwarth had an electricity cable taken through the centre of it in order to supply the organ!

Several of the old writers in the county mention hatchments where these no longer exist or are diminished. Cass in his book refers to 20 in East Barnet church of which only 10 remain today. A 19th-century engraving of St Albans Abbey shows several in the nave but not one has survived. The earliest hatchment appears to be for Edward Denny at Bishop's Stortford, 1720, and the latest for Dr. Perigal dated 1931 in Lyonsdown church in New Barnet.

There are several armorial boards in the county of various types, the most curious being in St Albans Abbey to the Maynard family; this is a board with three shields for families of Rowlatt, Seale and Maynard with their quarterings, dated 1547, 1613 and 1619, and is placed over the Maynard tomb.

It is surprising to find only one hatchment to the county's greatest family, the Cecils of Hatfield House, in Old Hatfield church. This one is for the Dowager Marchioness of Salisbury, known in court circles as 'Old Sarum'. She was Master of the Hatfield Hunt from 1793 until 1848, when she became too frail and blind to ride and gave up at the age of 77.

At Knebworth there is a hatchment to Lord Lytton, the famous Victorian novelist. Among the many memorials to the army and navy it is strange to find five to Admirals in close proximity, two at Broxbourne, one at East Barnet, one at Bengeo and one at Bushey.

A. W. Longden

(The late Bert Longden would, I am sure, have wished to acknowledge the help given by members of the Middlesex Heraldry Society and others who have checked every hatchment he recorded. Three hatchments have been added to the list, two at Cottered and one at Puttenham.   Ed.)

GREAT AMWELL

1. Dexter background black
Gules a chevron or between in chief two cinquefoils argent and in
base a buglehorn argent garnished and stringed or (Duncan), impaling,
Or a cross formy throughout double rebated between three pierced
molets azure (Mylne)
Crest: An East Indiaman in full sail proper, pennants at each
masthead and a flag at the stern gules   Mantling: Gules and argent
Motto: Disce pati   Flags in saltire behind shield
For William Duncan, late E. India Company's service, who m. Caroline,
dau. of Robert Mylne of Amwell, and d. 14 Mar. 1830, aged 83.
(Cussans, IX, 125-127; M.I.)
(Widow's hatchment is at Hitcham, Berkshire)

2. Dexter background black
Or a cross moline quarter-pierced between three molets azure (Mylne),
impaling, Per chevron argent and azure a chevron per chevron sable
and argent between in chief two roses gules barbed and seeded proper
and in base a garb or (Coxhead)
Crest: A bust of Minerva, vested vert, helmed argent, garnished or,
crested gules, over the crest the motto 'Tam arte quam marte'
Mantling: Gules and argent   Motto: Resurgam
For William Chadwell Mylne, F.R.S., architect and engineer, who m.
Mary, dau. of George Smith Coxhead, and d. Dec. 1863, aged 81. She
d. 10 Feb. 1874, aged 83.   (Cussans, IX, 125-127; M.I.)

BARKWAY

1. Dexter background black
Two shields   Dexter, within the ribbon of the Order of the Bath
and cross of Order pendent below, Argent six cross crosslets fitchy
sable, on a chief azure two molets or and a crescent argent for
difference (Clinton) ·   Sinister, within a wreath of laurel proper, as
dexter, impaling, Qly, 1st and 4th, Azure on a fess dancetty argent
between three griffins passant wings elevated or three escallops gules
(Holroyd), 2nd and 3rd, Azure three roses argent barbed and
seeded proper (   )
Crest: From a ducal coronet gules a plume of five feathers argent
Mantling: Gules and argent   Motto: Loyalte n'a honte
Supporters: Two greyhounds argent collared and lined gules, the
collars each charged with three crescents or

For General Sir William Henry Clinton, G.C.B., G.C.H., who m. 1797,
Louisa Dorothea, dau. of John, 1st Earl of Sheffield, and d. 16 Feb.
1846.   (B.P. 1875 ed.; M.I.)

2. All black background
Two shields, suspended from a knot of ribbons   Dexter, as 1, but
molets pierced   Sinister, on a cartouche within a gilt border, as 1.
Supporters: As 1.
For Louisa Dorothea, widow of General Sir William Henry Clinton,
who d. 14 May 1854.   (B.P. 1875 ed.; M.I.)

CHIPPING BARNET

1. Dexter background black
Argent an eagle displayed sable charged on the breast with an
escutcheon, Gules a bordure engrailed argent (Reid), impaling, to the
dexter, Qly 1st and 4th, Vert a lion rampant reguardant argent
between three arrows points downwards argent (Gildart), 2nd and 3rd,
Argent on a mount vert a savage ambulant between two oak trees,
wreathed at the temples and loins with oak leaves, in the dexter hand a
club resting on the shoulder, the sinister on his hip, all proper (Meyer),
impaling, to the sinister, Qly, 1st, Azure a lion rampant argent, 2nd,
Or a cubit arm issuant from the sinister vested gules cuffed argent
grasping in the hand proper a cross crosslet fitchy erect sable, 3rd, Or
a lymphad sails furled and oars in position sable, 4th, Per fess argent
and azure a rock proper (McNeill)
Crest: Out of a cloud proper an arm vested gules, cuffed argent,
holding a Bible proper, open at the Book of Job, ch. 19, leaves or
Mantling: Gules and argent   Motto: Pro virtuti
For Andrew Reid, who m. 1st, 1782, Harriet, dau. of Thomas Gildart,
of Moss Hall, Finchley, by his wife, Sarah Meyer. She d. 29 July 1802.
He m. 2nd, 1804, Janet McNeill, and d. 20 Apr. 1841.
(Cass, Vol. II, 162)

2. All black background
On a lozenge surmounted by a cherub's head   Argent an eagle
displayed sable charged on the breast with an escutcheon, Argent a
bordure engrailed gules (Reid), impaling, Qly, 1st, Azure a lion
rampant argent, 2nd, Or a cubit arm issuant from the sinister, the hand
proper grasping a cross crosslet fitchy erect azure, 3rd, Or a lymphad
sails furled and oars in position sable, 4th, Azure on a chief argent a
rock gules (McNeill)
For Janet, 2nd wife, and widow of Andrew Reid. She d. 16 Nov. 1842.
(Source, as 1.)

EAST BARNET

1. All black background
Per bend sinister ermine and sable ermined argent a lion rampant or
(Trevor)
Crest: On a chapeau gules and ermine a wyvern wings elevated sable
ducally gorged or   Mantling: Gules and argent   Motto: Mors
janua vitæ   Skull below shield
For Thomas Trevor of the Temple, b. 1684, grandson of Sir John
Trevor, Secretary of State to Charles II, d. unm. 6 Dec. 1741.
(Cass, E. Barnet)

2. All black background
On a lozenge surmounted by a cherub's head   Trevor, as 1.
Motto: In coelo quies   Skull below shield
For Arabella Trevor, niece of Thomas Trevor, b. 1714, d. unm. 1789.
(Source, as 1.)

3. All black background
Gules a lion rampant within an orle of eight cross crosslets fitchy
argent (Warre)
Crest: From a ducal coronet or a griffin's head argent
Mantling: Gules and argent   Motto: In coelo quies
Union Jacks and other flags in saltire behind shield, also cannons; five
cannon balls below shield and an anchor
For Rear-Admiral Henry Warre, R.N., b. 13 Sept. 1735, d. 22 Nov.
1826.   (B.L.G. 1937 ed.; Cass; M.I.)

4. Sinister background black
Per pale sable and gules gutty argent a lion rampant or ermined sable
(Kingston) impaling, Qly ermine and paly of six or and gules (Knightley)
Motto: In coelo quies   Two cherubs' heads above shield
For Jane, dau. of Valentine Knightley, M.P., of Fawsley, Northants,
who m. John Kingston, of East Barnet, and d. 3 July 1810.
(Source, as 1.)

5. Dexter background black
Sable on a chevron engrailed ermine between three lions rampant or a
bee proper between two bezants, on a chief argent three horseshoes
sable (Wyatt), impaling, Argent on a bend cotised azure three lozenges
ermine (Reeves)
Crest: An ostrich gules charged on the wings with ten bezants, in the
beak a horseshoe sable   Mantling: Gules and argent   Motto:
Suivez raison
For Thomas Wyatt, of Willenhall House, East Barnet, who m. Elizabeth
Reeves, and d. 6 Apr. 1834, aged 51. She d. 12 May 1867, aged 74.
(Source, as 1.)

6. All black background
On a lozenge surmounted by a cherub's head   Qly, 1st, Argent a
bend engrailed between six martlets sable (Tempest), 2nd, Per chevron
argent and sable in chief two pierced molets and in base a heathcock
counterchanged (Heath), 3rd, Sable a talbot passant within a bordure
engrailed argent (Sudbury), 4th, Azure a maunch argent within a
bordure argent charged with eight pairs of lions' gambs erased
saltirewise gules (Wharton), impaling, Azure a chevron ermine between
three escallops argent (Townsend)
Motto: Resurgam
For Anne, dau. of Joseph Townsend, of Honington Hall, Warwick,
who m. John Tempest, of Wynyard and Brancepeth Castle, M.P. for
Durham, and d. 31 July 1817, aged 61. He d. 3 Aug. 1794.
(B.P. 1939 ed.; Cass)

7. Dexter background black
Qly, 1st, Per fess azure and or a pale counterchanged and three bucks'
heads erased or (Roper), 2nd, Or on a fess gules three fleurs-de-lys or
(Lennard), 3rd, Gules three escallops argent (Dacre), 4th, Per bend
sinister ermine and sable ermined argent (Trevor)   In pretence:
Sable a cross moline or between four escallops argent each charged
with a cross moline sable (Fludyer)
Baron's coronet   Crest: A lion rampant sable holding in its
forepaws a ducal coronet or   Motto: Spes mea in Deo
Supporters: Dexter, A wolf argent gorged with a spiked collar and
chained or   Sinister, A bull gules ducally gorged and chained or
All on a mantle gules and ermine
For Trevor Charles, 18th Lord Dacre, who m. Mary, only dau. and heir
of Sir Thomas Fludyer, and d.s.p. 4 July 1794. She d. 11 Sept. 1808.
(B.P. 1939 ed.)

8. Dexter background black
Per chevron or and ermine, on a chevron sable between in chief two
eagles' heads erased gules and in base a garb or a harrow or between
two fountains (Cass), impaling, Sable a fess ermine between three
cinquefoils argent (Potter)
Crest: An eagle's head erased gules charged on the neck with a fountain,
in the beak three ears of wheat or   Mantling: Sable and or
Motto: Ubique patriam reminisci
For Frederick Cass, J.P., D.L., of Little Grove, East Barnet, who m.
1823, Martha, eldest dau. of John Dell Potter, of Ponders End, and d.
17 May 1861, aged 73. She d. 29 June 1870.
(Burke's Family Records; Cass; M.I.)

9. Sinister background black
Qly of eight, 1st and 8th, Sable a lion passant argent, on a chief argent
three cross crosslets sable (Long), 2nd, Per fess or and gules a pale

counterchanged and three choughs proper, a molet argent in centre
chief for cadency (Tate), 3rd, Gules twelve bezants three, three, three,
two and one, and a canton ermine (Zouch), 4th, Argent two chevronels
gules in chief a label of three points azure (St Maur), 5th, Gules three
leopards' faces jessant-de-lys reversed or (Cantelupe), 6th, Or a cross
patonce vert (Daubeney), 7th, Or fretty gules a canton ermine (Noel)
In pretence: Per pale gules and azure on a chevron argent between
three martlets or an eagle displayed sable (Beckford)
Motto: Resurgam   Cherubs' heads above shield, which is
suspended from a lover's knot
For Mary, dau. and heir of Thomas Beckford, who m. Edward Long,
barrister at Gray's Inn, and d. 16 Jan. 1797, aged 62.
(B.L.G. 2nd ed.; Cass; M.I.)

10. Sinister background black
Qly, 1st, Long (lion holds a cross crosslet fitchy or in dexter paw),
2nd, Tate (no cadency mark), 3rd, Zouch (ten bezants, four, three, two
and one), 4th, Beckford
In pretence: Per pale argent and azure three greyhounds courant in
pale counterchanged, on a chief azure a fret or (Thomlinson)
Motto: Pieux quoique preux   Cherubs' heads above shield, which
is suspended from a lover's knot
For Mary, only child of John Thomlinson, M.P. for Steyning, who m.
Edward Beeston Long, of Hampton Lodge, Farnham, and d. 16 Mar.
1818. He d. 17 Sept. 1825, aged 62.   (B.L.G. 2nd ed.; Cass; M.I.)

NEW BARNET, Holy Trinity, Lyonsdown

1. All black background
Per fess gules and vert, in chief a dexter mailed gauntlet argent lined
gules in bend sinister grasping a sword in bend point upwards argent
pommelled and hilted or; in base a cock argent on its back head to
dexter side, wattled and combed gules, beaked, legged and spurred or,
its entrails issuant to sinister gules (Perigal)
No crest, but a five-barred helm affronté or lined gules
Mantling: Gules and argent   To dexter and sinister the dates, 1848
and 1931   On a scroll below the word Peri-Gal
For Arthur Perigal, M.D., of Lismore House, New Barnet, who d. 1931.
(Kelly's Directory, 1925; date on hatchment)

BENGEO

1. All black background
Azure on a chevron or between three bears' heads couped argent

muzzled gules a buck's head erased proper between two hands couped
at the wrist proper each grasping a dagger argent hilted or (Mackay)
Baron's coronet   Crest: A hand proper couped at the wrist grasping
a dagger erect argent hilted or   Motto: Manu forti
Supporters: Two soldiers in 19th century uniforms, red with white
facings, epaulettes and crossbelts, breeches white, boots and leggings
black, busby black with white hackle, each holding a musket armed
with a bayonet in the exterior hand
For Eric, 7th Baron Reay, who d. unm. at Goldings, Herts, 7 July 1847,
aged 73.   (B.P. 1875 ed.)

2. Sinister background black
Gules a chevron between three crescents ermine (Gosselin)   In
pretence: Gules on a chevron or three cross crosslets sable (Hadsley)
Motto: Resurgam   Two cherubs' heads at top corners of shield
which is suspended by ribbons tied with a lover's knot
For Sarah, dau. of Jeremiah Rayment Hadsley, of Ware Priory, who
m. 1809, Rear Admiral Thomas le Marchant Gosselin, of Bengeo
Hall, and d. 20 Nov. 1815, aged 39.
(B.L.G. 5th ed.; gravestone in churchyard)

3. All black background
Arms: As 2.
Crest: A blackamoor's head in profile proper, wreathed at the temples
with ribbons argent and gules tied behind the head, and a gold
earring pendent from the ear lobe   Mantling: Gules and argent
Motto: Resurgam
For Thomas le Marchant Gosselin, of Bengeo Hall, Senior Admiral of
Her Majesty's Navy, who d. 27 Nov. 1857, aged 92.   (Sources, as 2.)

BERKHAMSTED

1. All black background
Or on a chevron cotised between three demi-griffins the two in chief
respectant sable a leopard's face or (Smith), impaling, Gules a lion
rampant or, on a chief or three sprigs of laurel vert (Pechell)
Crest: A elephant's head erased or   Mantling: Gules and argent
Motto: The righteous hath hope in his death
For James Smith, who m. 2nd, 1803, Mary Isabella, dau. of Augustus
Pechell, and d. 16 Feb. 1843.   (B.L.G. 5th ed.; M.I.)

2. All black background
On a lozenge surmounted by a cherub's head
Pechell   In pretence: Qly, 1st and 4th, Argent a wyvern passant
wings addorsed and tail nowed gules (Drake), 2nd and 3rd, Gules a
fess chequy or and sable (   )

Motto: Resurgam
For Sarah, 3rd dau. and co-heir of the Rev. Thomas Drake, Rector of
Amersham, who m. 1786, Augustus Pechell, and d. 20 Jan. 1839.
(B.P. 1939 ed.; M.I.)

3. Dexter background black
Pechell, impaling, Azure on a fess between three molets or three signs
of the planet Venus sable (Thoyts)
Crest: A lark proper   Mantling: Gules and argent   Motto:
Resurgam
For Samuel George Pechell, Capt. R.N., who m. 1817, Caroline, 2nd
dau. of William Thoyts, of Sulhampstead House, Berks, and d. 30
Dec. 1840.   (B.P. 1939 ed.; M.I.)

4. Dexter background black
Sable a cross engrailed argent between four lions' heads erased argent
crowned or (   ), impaling to dexter, Argent a lion rampant gules
crowned or between three escallops sable (   ), and to sinister,
Sable a stag's head cabossed between two flaunches argent (Parker)
Crest: A lion's head erased argent crowned or   Mantling: Gules and
argent   Motto: Resurgam
Unidentified

BISHOP'S STORTFORD

1. Dexter background black
Sable a saltire argent, the Badge of Ulster (Duckett), impaling, Qly,
1st and 4th, Or on a pile gules between six fleurs-de-lys azure three
lions passant guardant in pale or (Seymour Augmentation), 2nd
and 3rd, Gules two wings conjoined in lure points downward or
(Seymour)
Crest: From a ducal coronet or a plume of five feathers argent
Motto: Je vieux le droit   Supporters: Two popinjays wings
displayed proper
For Sir George Duckett, 2nd Bt., who m. 2nd, 1846, Charlotte, dau. of
Edmond Seymour, of Inholmes, Berkshire, and d. 15 June 1856.
(B.P. 1875 ed.)

2. All black background
Gules a saltire argent between twelve crosses formy or (Denny)
Crest: A cubit arm vested per pale gules and or, cuffed argent, the
hand proper grasping five stalks of wheat or   Mantling: Gules and
argent   Motto: In caelo quies
Probably for Edward Denny, who d. 14 Mar. 1720, aged 90.   (M.I.)

BROXBOURNE

1. All black background

Qly, 1st and 4th, Azure three lozenges or (Freeman), 2nd and 3rd,
Gules a wolf reguardant argent issuing from a cave on the sinister or
(Williams), impaling, Gules two chevrons the upper or the lower argent
(Wills)
Crests: Dexter, A demi-lion rampant gules charged on the shoulder
with a lozenge or   Sinister, A lion rampant proper crowned or
Mantling: Gules and argent   Motto: Resurgam   Behind the shield
are four flags, two red and two white ensigns, naval guns and an anchor
For Admiral of the Fleet William Peere Williams-Freeman, who m.
Henrietta Wills, and d. at Hoddesdon, 11 Feb. 1832, aged 91. She d. 3
Sept. 1819, aged 73.   (Cussans, IX, 187–195)

2. All black background

Azure a lion rampant or, on a canton argent three lions passant two
and one sable (   ), impaling to dexter, Gules three garbs within a
bordure engrailed or (Kemp), and to sinister, Argent a cross azure
between four billets sable, on a chief azure a rose argent between two
fleurs-de-lys or (Morritt)
Crest: A lion passant sable charged with a portcullis argent
Mantling: Gules and argent   Motto: Resurgemus   Flags and
cannon behind shield
Unidentified

3. Dexter background black

Gules three lions passant guardant per pale or and argent (O'Brien),
impaling, Gules on a chief ermine a trefoil slipped vert between two
roundels azure (Walmsley)
Crest: From a cloud argent an arm in armour embowed the hand
holding a dagger fesswise proper pommelled or   Mantling: Gules
and argent   Motto: Vigeur de dessus   Blue and red ensigns and
cannon behind shield
For Rear-Admiral Donat Hoste O'Brien of Hoddesdon, who m. Hannah,
dau. of John Walmsley, of Rochdale, and d. 13 May 1857, aged 72.
(Source, as 1.)

4. All black background

On a lozenge surmounted by a cherub's head
Arms: As 3, but no trefoil   Motto: Resurgam
For Hannah, widow of Admiral Donat Hoste O'Brien. She d. 5 Oct.
1863, aged 60.   (Source, as 1.)

5. Dexter background black

Or a saltire between four molets sable (Christie), impaling, Gules three
hawks' lures argent, chain and bell or (Falconer)

Crest: A holly tree proper   Mantling: Gules and argent   Motto:
Sic viresco
For William Christie, of Hoddesdon, who m. Margaret Falconer, and
d. 14 Oct. 1811, aged 67. She d. 1 Feb. 1844, aged 85.   (Source, as 1.)

6. Dexter background black
Azure crusilly a lion rampant argent a chief barry nebuly of four sable
and argent (Dalton), impaling, Paly of six argent and azure, on a
chief or a lion passant guardant gules (   )
Crest: A dragon's head azure wings elevated or undersides gules
collared nebuly argent   Mantling: Gules and argent   Motto: In
coelo quies   Painted on frame: Francis Dalton, Esq.
For Francis Dalton, who d. 30 Nov. 1819, aged 49.   (Source, as 1.)

7. Dexter background black
Azure a chevron humetty between three covered cups or, in chief a
crescent argent for difference (Christian), impaling, Gules on a chief
ermine two roundels azure (Walmsley)
Crest: A unicorn's head erased argent, maned and tufted or
Mantling: Gules and argent   Motto: Quies in coelo
For Edward Christian, chief justiciary of the Isle of Ely, who m. Mary,
dau. of John Walmsley, and d. 29 Mar. 1823, aged 63.
(Source, as 1; M.I.)

8. All black background
On a lozenge surmounted by a cherub's head
Azure a chevron between three covered cups or in a chief a crescent
argent for difference (Christian), impaling, Gules on a chief ermine a
trefoil slipped or between two roundels azure (Walmsley)
Motto: Resurgam
For Mary, widow of Edward Christian. She d. 8 Jan. 1824, aged 55.
(Source, as 1.)

BUSHEY

1. All black background
Qly, 1st and 4th, Paly of six argent and azure, on a chief argent three
lions' heads erased sable (   ), 2nd and 3rd, Sable a pile engrailed
ermine (   )   In pretence: Or a pale between four fleurs-de-lys
gules (   )
Crest: Out of a ducal coronet or a lion's head erased sable
Mantling: Gules and argent   Motto: Resurgam
Unidentified

2. All black background
On a lozenge surmounted by a cherub's head   Ermine two bars
gemel azure, on a chief gules a leopard passant guardant or spotted
sable (Isherwood)
Motto: In coelo quies
Unidentified

3. Dexter background black
Two shields   Dexter, surrounded with the Order of the Bath, Per
fess argent and sable a fess per fess counter-embattled between
three falcons all counterchanged, in centre chief the Badge of Ulster
(Thompson)   Sinister, within an ornamental wreath, Thompson,
impaling, Argent a chevron sable ermined or between three griffins'
heads erased sable (Raikes)
Crest: Out of a naval crown or, sails argent, an arm embowed in
armour argent the hand grasping a spear erect or point argent
Mantling: Sable and argent   Motto: Non quo sed quomodo
Supporters: Dexter, An eagle wings elevated and addorsed murally
crowned or   Sinister, A sailor in 19th century dress, shirt and
trousers white, jacket blue, hat, scarf and boots black, holding
in his exterior hand a staff bearing a pennant argent with a cross of St
George in the part next the staff and the word NILE sable in the fly
For Admiral Sir Thomas Boulden Thompson, 1st Bt., G.C.B., who
m. 1799, Anne, eldest dau. of Robert Raikes, of Gloucester, and d. 3
Mar. 1828. She d. 9 Sept. 1846.   (B.P. 1949 ed.)

4. Sinister background black
A shield and a lozenge   Dexter, shield, Argent on a chief gules a
cushion between two molets of six points argent pierced gules
(Marjoribanks), impaling, Argent on a chevron sable, between three
roundels sable, the two in chief charged with a martlet and the one in
base with a trefoil slipped argent, three mascles argent (Pratt)
Sinister, lozenge, Qly per pale wavy argent and or, in the first and
fourth two wings bendwise in pale azure each charged with a trefoil
slipped or, in the second and third a tree eradicated proper charged on
the foliage with a shield bendwise gules thereon three gouttes or
(Thellusson), impaling, Pratt   Shield surmounted with an
esquire's helm and the lozenge with a baroness's coronet
Supporters (to lozenge): Two greyhounds reguardant argent collared
azure
For Lucy, 3rd dau. of Edward Roger Pratt of Ryston Hall, Norfolk,
relict of William, 3rd Baron Rendlesham, who m. 1841, Stewart
Marjoribanks, of Bushey Grove, and d. 12 May 1854.   (B.P. 1875 ed.)

5. All black background
A shield and a lozenge   Dexter, shield, Argent on a chief gules a
cushion between two molets of eight points argent pierced gules,

at honour point a molet sable for difference (Marjoribanks), impaling, Pratt, as 4, but martlets and trefoil or   Sinister, lozenge, surmounted with a baroness's coronet, Thellusson, but per pale plain not wavy, impaling, Pratt, as dexter
Crest (above shield): A lion's gamb erased or grasping a tilting spear in bend sinister or point downwards argent   Motto (below shield): Advance with courage   Supporters (to lozenge): As 4.
For Stewart Marjoribanks, of Bushey Grove, who d. Sept. 1863. (B.P. 1875 ed.)

COTTERED

1. Sinister background black
Gules a chevron between three mallets or (Soames)   In pretence: Gules a bezant between three crescents all within a bordure engrailed ermine (Alden)
Motto: In coelo quies
Shield flanked by cherubs' heads and bow of ribbon above
Probably for Elizabeth, wife of Henry Soames. She d. 6 Jan. 1821. (M.I.)

2. All black background
Arms: As 1.
Crest: A lure gules, standing thereon a falcon close or   Mantling: Gules and argent   Motto: Resurgam
Probably for Henry Soames, widower, who d. 13 Nov. 1839.   (M.I.)

FLAMSTEAD

1. Dexter background black
Qly, 1st and 4th, Argent three cinquefoils sable (Sebright), 2nd, Per chevron sable and argent three elephants' heads erased counterchanged (Saunders), 3rd, Or a saltire gules over all a fess sable (Ashe), over all the Badge of Ulster, impaling, Argent three pallets gules within a bordure engrailed sable, on a canton argent a spur rowel to base and leathered gules (Knight)
Crest: A heraldic tyger sejant argent, maned and tufted or, langued gules, crowned or   Mantling: Gules and argent   Motto: Resurgam
For Sir John Sebright, 6th Bt., who m. 1766, Sarah, dau. of Edward Knight of Wolverley, co. Worcs, and d. 23 Feb. 1794.   (B.P. 1949 ed.)
(This hatchment is now missing; there is another hatchment for Sir John at Besford, Worcestershire)

2. All black background

On a lozenge surmounted by a cherub's head   Qly, 1st and 4th, Sebright, 2nd, Per chevron gules and argent three elephants' heads erased counterchanged (Saunders), 3rd, Argent a saltire gules over all a fess sable (Ashe), in centre chief the Badge of Ulster, impaling, Argent three pallets gules within a bordure engrailed azure, on a canton gules a spur rowel to base and leathered or (Knight)
Motto: Resurgam
For Sarah, widow of Sir John Sebright, 6th Bt. She was bur. 4 Jan. 1813.   (B.P. 1949 ed.)

3. All black background

Qly, 1st, Sebright, with Badge of Ulster, 2nd, Azure six bezants, three, two and one (Ramsey), 3rd, Or a saltire gules over all a fess sable (Ashe), 4th, Saunders, as 1.   In pretence: Or three bulls' heads couped at the neck sable (Crofts)
Crest and mantling: As 1.   Motto: Servare mentem
For Sir John Saunders Sebright, 7th Bt., who m. 1793, Harriet, only dau. and heiress of Richard Crofts, of West Harling, Norfolk, and d. 15 Apr. 1846. She d. Aug. 1826.   (B.P. 1949 ed.)

4. Sinister background black

On a lozenge suspended from a lover's knot   Sebright, with Badge of Ulster, impaling, Per pale dancetty gules and vert, on a chief or a lion passant sable armed and langued gules (Henry)
For Olivia, youngest dau. of Joseph Henry, of Straffan, co. Kildare, who m. as his 2nd wife, Sir Thomas Gage Saunders Sebright, 8th Bt., and d. 27 June 1859.   (B.P. 1949 ed.)

5. All black background

Arms: As 4, but chief argent
Crest: As 1.   Mantling: Sable and argent   Motto: Servare mentem
For Sir Thomas Gage Saunders Sebright, 8th Bt., who d. 29 Aug. 1864. (B.P. 1949 ed.)

6. All black background

Vert a fess between three garbs or (   )
Crest: A stag's head erased argent attired or   Mantling: Gules and argent   Motto: Resurgam
Unidentified

7. Dexter background black

Azure two chevronels between three boars' heads couped close and erased or (Cotin), impaling, Argent a saltire engrailed gules (   )
Crest: A boar's head argent   Mantling: Gules and argent
Motto: Resurgam   Winged skull below
Unidentified

8. Dexter background black
Sable two bars or a canton ermine (Westcomb), impaling, Argent on a
chevron engrailed azure between three martlets sable three crescents
or (Watson)
Crest: From a mural coronet a griffin's head or   Mantling: Gules
and argent   Motto: Mors janua vitæ   Skull below
For William Westcomb of Cheverells Green, who d. 26 Sept. 1757,
aged 70. His wife Elizabeth d. 15 July 1767.   (Cussans, XIII, 111;
M.I. in churchyard)

HATFIELD

1. All black background
Shield and lozenge, the sinister partly surmounting dexter
Dexter, within the Garter, Barry of ten argent and azure, on each of
six escutcheons three, two and one sable a lion rampant argent (Cecil)
Sinister, Cecil, impaling, Sable on a fess between three leopards passant
guardant argent, spotted sable, three escallops gules (Hill)
Marchioness's coronet   Supporters: Two lions guardant ermine
On a mantle gules and argent
For Mary Amelia, dau. of Wills, 1st Marquess of Downshire, who m.
James, 1st Marquess of Salisbury, and d. 27 Nov. 1835. He d. 13 June
1823.   (B.P. 1949 ed.)

HEMEL HEMPSTEAD

1. Dexter background black
Qly of eight, 1st and 4th, Vert a lion rampant argent armed and langued
gules (Hume), 2nd and 3rd, Or three popinjays vert beaked and legged
gules (Pepdie), 5th, Or three piles engrailed issuing from the chief gules
(Polwarth) 6th and 7th, Gyronny of eight or and sable (Campbell),
8th, Argent a cross engrailed azure (St Clair) in centre of dexter, an
escutcheon argent charged with an orange stalked and leaved ensigned
with an imperial crown proper, a coat of Augmentation by William III,
impaling, Vert on a chief embattled or three pheons points
downwards vert (Crompton) Earl's coronet
Crest: Out of a human heart gules a dexter arm couped at the elbow
holding a scimitar proper   Mantling: Gules and argent   Motto:
Fides coronat probata   Supporters: Two lions rampant reguardant
argent langued gules
For Hugh, 3rd Earl of Marchmont, who m. Elizabeth, dau. of Windmill
Crompton, and d. 10 Jan. 1794.   (B.P. 1949 ed.)
(In poor condition, and in urgent need of repair)

2. All black background
On a lozenge surmounted by a countess's coronet
Arms: As 1.
Motto and supporters: As 1.
For Elizabeth, widow of Hugh, 3rd Earl of Marchmont. She d. 12
Feb. 1797.   (B.P. 1949 ed.)

3. Sinister background black
Qly, 1st and 4th, Vert a fess embattled or between in chief two pheons
and in base two thigh bones in saltire argent (Cooper), 2nd, Argent
on a bend cotised sable between two fleurs-de-lys azure a lion passant
argent (Bransby), 3rd, Azure six fleurs-de-lys three, two and one or, a
chief indented or (Paston), over all the Badge of Ulster, impaling,
Argent three cocks gules, on a chief gules two bucks passant or (Cocks)
Motto: Resurgam   Cherub's head above
For Anne, dau. of Thomas Cocks, who m. 1792, as his 1st wife, Sir
Astley Paston Cooper, 1st Bt., and d. 10 June 1827.   (B.P. 1949 ed.)

4. Dexter background black
Two shields   Dexter, within Order of Hanover, the cross pendent
between the shields, Cooper with Badge of Ulster in centre chief
Sinister, Cooper, impaling, Argent a chevron indented gules between
three boars' heads couped close sable, langued and tusked gules (Jones)
Crest: From a mural coronet or in front of a demi-spear erect proper,
head argent and tasselled or, two palm branches in saltire proper
Mantling: Gules and or   Motto: Nil magnum nisi bonum
For Sir Astley Paston Cooper, 1st Bt., who m. 2nd, Catherine, dau. of
J. Jones, of Derry Ormond Park, co. Cardigan, and d. 12 Feb. 1841.
(B.P. 1949 ed.)

5. Dexter background black
Cooper, in chief the Badge of Ulster, impaling, Sable a fess indented
and in chief two eagles displayed or (Rickford)
Crest: As 4.   Mantling: Vert and or   Motto: As 4.
For Sir Astley Paston Cooper, 2nd Bt., who m. 1821, Elizabeth
Harriet, dau. of William Rickford, and d. 6 Jan. 1866.   (B.P. 1949 ed.)

HEXTON

1. Dexter background black
Or ermined sable a fess embattled cotised gules, in chief a tower sable
(de Latour)   In pretence: Azure a martlet between three molets
pierced or within a bordure invected compony argent and gules
(Young)
Crest: From a coronet of nine points or crowned with pearls a cubit

arm vambraced sable garnished or holding a shield pendent to dexter
azure charged with a tower argent   Mantling: Gules and or
Motto: Pour Dieu et mon Pays   Supporters: Two angels dressed in
white tunics reaching to mid-thigh and across the breast a scarf
bendwise azure, the sinister angel with scarf over the sinister shoulder
For Joseph Andrew De Latour, who m. Caroline, heiress of William
Young, Lord of the Manor of Hexton, and d. 28 Mar. 1845, in Paris,
buried in Hexton, 12 Apr. 1845.   (M.I.; Cussans, VII)

HITCHIN

1. Dexter background black
Gules a chevron between three hinds trippant or (Hinde), impaling,
Argent a chevron between three fireballs sable fired proper (Ball)
Crest: None   Mantling: Gules and argent   Motto: In coelo quies
Skull in base
For Robert Hinde, of Hunsdon House, Herts, eldest son of Robert
Hinde, of Chertsey, and Abryana, dau. of John Venables, who m.
Mary, dau. of Thomas Ball, Governor of Jersey, and d. 29 Sept. 1786.
(M.I.; Cussans, VII, 71)

2. All black background
On a lozenge surmounted by a cherub's head
Qly of six, 1st and 5th, Hinde, 2nd and 6th, Sable on a chevron
between three castles argent three leopards' faces gules (Hardcastle),
3rd and 4th, Azure two bars argent (Venables), impaling, Argent a
chevron between three fireballs sable fired in four places proper (Ball)
Motto: Resurgam
For Mary, widow of Robert Hinde. She d. 14 Feb. 1819.   (M.I.)

3. All black background
On a lozenge surmounted by a cherub's head
Qly, as 2.
Motto: Resurgam
Probably for Mary Elizabeth Hinde, d. 23 Feb. 1816, Catherine
Amelia Hinde, d. 6 Jan. 1813, or Charlotte Hinde, d. 7 Sept. 1846.
(M.I.s)

ICKLEFORD

1. All black background
Argent three cocks gules (Cockayne), impaling, Gules a chevron
engrailed between three owls argent (Hewitt)

Crest: A cock's head gules   Mantling: Gules and argent, enclosing
two cherubs' heads   Motto: Resurgam
For Thomas Cockayne, of Ickleford, who m. 1787, Susan, dau. of
James Hewitt, of Dublin, and d. 14 Oct. 1809, aged 51. She d. 10
Jan. 1790, aged 23.   (M.I.)

2. Sinister background black
Cockayne, impaling, Or a chevron sable ermined or between three
boars passant sable (   )
Two cherubs' heads above
Probably for Marian Amelia, widow of George Edwards, who m.
Thomas Cockayne, son of Thomas Cockayne (No. 1), and d. 25 Nov.
1821, aged 26. He d. 26 May 1852, aged 62.   (M.I.; Cussans, VII, 30)

KING'S WALDEN

1. Dexter and top sinister background black
Azure a chevron embattled or (Hale), impaling two coats per fess, in
chief, Argent on a cross sable nine gouttes or (Leeson), and in base,
Per fess or and the base per pale dexter vert and sinister per pale
argent and sable, in chief a dexter hand couped at the wrist and gloved
holding a rod entwined with a serpent proper between two lions
rampant respectant gules, in dexter base a buck trippant or, and in
sinister base a boar passant counterchanged (Sullivan)
Crest: Six arrows points downwards enlaced by a serpent vert
Mantling: Gules and argent   Motto: Resurgam
For William Hale, of King's Walden, who m. 1st, 1815, Elizabeth, only
dau. of the Hon. William Leeson, of Codicote. She d. 11 Apr. 1823,
aged 26. He m. 2nd, 1824, Charlotte, eldest dau. of Sir Richard Joseph
Sullivan, 1st Bt. of Thames Ditton, and d. 21 Feb. 1852.
(M.I.; B.L.G. 1894 ed.; Cussans, VII, 122, 123)

KNEBWORTH

1. Dexter background black
Qly, 1st and 4th, Qly argent and gules in the second and third quarters
a fret or over all a fess azure (Norreys), 2nd and 3rd, Ermine on a
chief indented azure three ducal coronets or (Lytton)   In pretence:
Argent two bars sable (Brereton)
Crest: On a mound vert a chough rising proper   Mantling: Gules and
argent   Motto: In coelo quies   Skull below

For John Robinson-Lytton, who m. 1744, Leonora, dau. and heir of
Humphrey Brereton, of Borras, co. Denbigh, and d.s.p. 12 Apr. 1762.
(B.P. 1949 ed.)

2. Dexter background black
Qly, 1st and 4th, Lytton, 2nd, Argent a chevron sable between three
choughs proper (Warburton), 3rd, Norreys, impaling, Sable ermined
argent a trefoil slipped or between three round buckles tongues pendent
argent (Jodrell)
Crest and mantling: As 1.   Motto: Resurgam   Skull below
For Richard Warburton Lytton, son of William Warburton and Barbara,
dau of William Robinson-Lytton, m. 1768, Elizabeth, dau. of Paul
Jodrell, of Lewknor, and d. 29 Dec. 1810.   (B.P. 1949 ed.)

3. All black background
On a lozenge   Qly of six, 1st, qly i. & iv. Gules a chevron between
three eagles close reguardant or (Bulwer), ii. & iii. Per fess azure and or
in chief a dove argent and in base three molets sable (Wiggett), 2nd,
Gules a chevron argent between three eagles close reguardant or
(Bulwer), 3rd, Gules a cross moline argent between four lions' heads
erased or (Beck), 4th, Argent on a bend sable three wolves' heads
erased argent within a bordure engrailed gules bezanty (Yonge),
5th, Azure a fess between two bars gemel argent (Earle), 6th, Argent
three towers gules (Castell)   In pretence: Qly, 1st and 4th, Lytton,
with a canton argent charged with a rose gules for Strode, 2nd and
3rd, Norreys
For Elizabeth Barbara, dau. and heir of Richard Warburton Lytton,
who m. 1798, Brig. General William Earle Bulwer, of Wood Dalling and
Heydon, and d. 19 Dec. 1842.   (B.P. 1949 ed.)
(The hatchment of her husband, who d. 7 July 1807, is at Guestwick,
Norfolk)

4. All black background
Qly of six, 1st and 6th, qly i. & iv. Lytton with canton, as 3, ii. & iii.
Bulwer, over all the Badge of Ulster (1st quarter only), 2nd, Bulwer,
3rd, Azure a fess or between two bars gemel argent (Earle), 4th,
Warburton, 5th, Norreys, with crescent argent for difference   Shield
surrounded with the collar of the Order of St Michael and St George
Baron's coronet   Crests: Dexter, A bittern in flags proper charged
with a rose gules   Sinister, A heraldic tyger's head erased ermine
crined and armed or   Motto: Hoc virtutis opus   Supporters:
Two angels proper
For Edward George Earle Lytton-Bulwer, 1st Baron Lytton, the
author, who d. 18 Jan. 1873.   (B.P. 1949 ed.)

LILLEY

1. All black background

Barry of six sable and gules on a chevron between three lions rampant argent three annulets gules (Sowerby)
Crest: A lion rampant argent   Mantling: Gules and argent
Motto: Resurgam
Probably for William Sowerby, b. 1776, d. unm. 1838.
(B.L.G. 1937 ed.; M.I.; Cussans, VII)

LITTLE MUNDEN

1. All black background

Qly, 1st and 4th, Gules a cross patonce argent, on a chief vert a lion passant or (Chauncy), 2nd and 3rd, Qly gules and azure a cross flory or between four molets argent (Snell), impaling, Sable on a chevron or between three griffins' heads argent three estoiles gules (Beale)
Crests: Dexter, from a ducal coronet or a griffin's head vert charged with two pallets gules between two wings displayed azure, the inner sides of the wings charged with three pallets gules (Chauncy)
Sinister, A wolf statant or on a lamb couchant argent in front of a cross formy fitchy argent (Snell)
Mantling: Gules and argent   Motto: Sublimis per ardua tendo
For Charles Snell-Chauncy, of Dane End, Little Munden, who m. 1817, Elizabeth, dau. of Daniel Beale, of Fitzroy Square, London, and d. 9 Oct. 1866.   (M.I.; B.L.G. 1894 ed.; Cussans, XI, 152, 153)

PUTTENHAM

1. All black background

Two shields, each within a laurel wreath   Dexter, Qly, 1st and 4th, Gules a chevron between three leopards' faces or (Parker), 2nd, Ermine a bend between two cocks gules (Law), 3rd, Or two chevrons gules (Macklellan)   Sinister, as dexter, impaling, Per bend sinister sable and argent a lion rampant gutty between six cross crosslets fitchy, all counterchanged (   )
Knight's helm   Three crests: Centre, Issuant from a ducal coronet a leopard's face or   Dexter, A naked arm holding a sword erect proper hilted or, thereon a Moor's face proper   Sinister, A unicorn's head erased argent armed and crined or   Mottoes: (above dexter crest)   Nec obscura   (above sinister) Think on   Mantling: Gules and argent   Motto: (below shield) Dum spiro spero

The following decorations are pendent below the dexter shield:
Davison's Nile medal, the Spanish Order of Charles III, the Portuguese
Order of Christ, the Prussian Order of the Black Eagle, and a
Turkish Order
Possibly for Lt. William Parker, who m. Anne, and d. 24 July
1862.   (Naval Records, P.R.O., Kew)

REDBOURN

1. All black background
Qly, 1st and 4th, Argent on a fess sable three estoiles of six points or,
in chief an ermine spot (Grimston), 2nd and 3rd, Sable a fess indented,
in chief a leopard's face or (Luckyn), in chief the Badge of Ulster
In pretence: Qly, 1st and 4th, Azure a fess indented or between three
eagles displayed argent (Walter), 2nd and 3rd, two coats per pale,
Argent three bugle horns sable stringed gules (Forrester), Azure three
bars indented or (   )
Viscount's coronet   Crest: A stag's head couped proper
Motto: Mediocria firma   Supporters: Dexter, A stag reguardant
proper   Sinister, A griffin reguardant or   All on a mantle
gules and ermine
For James Bucknall, 3rd Viscount Grimston, who m. 1774, Harriot,
only dau. and heiress of Edward Walter, of Stalbridge, Dorset, and d. 1
Jan. 1809.   (B.P. 1949 ed.)
(The hatchment of Lady Grimston is at Gorhambury)

2. Dexter background black
Qly of six, 1st, Argent on a fess sable three pierced molets of six
points or, in dexter chief an ermine spot and in sinister chief the Badge
of Ulster (Grimston), 2nd, Sable a fess dancetty between two
leopards' faces or (Luckyn), 3rd, Argent two chevrons gules between
three stags' heads cabossed proper (Bucknall), 4th, Argent a fess
dancetty per pale azure and gules between three eagles displayed sable
(Walter), 5th, Argent a fess gules between three bugle horns sable
stringed gules (Forrester), 6th, Gules a quatrefoil or (Rowe),
impaling, Azure on a fess wavy argent a cross formy gules, in chief two
pierced molets of six points or (Jenkinson)
Earl's coronet   Crest: A stag's head erased proper attired or
Motto: Mediocria firma   Supporters: Dexter, A stag reguardant
proper attired or   Sinister, A griffin reguardant or
For James Walter, 1st Earl of Verulam, who m. 1807, Charlotte, dau.
of Charles, 1st Earl of Liverpool, and d. 17 Nov. 1845.
(B.P. 1949 ed.)

RIDGE

1. Dexter background black
Two shields   Dexter, within the Garter, Argent on a saltire azure
a bezant (Yorke)   Sinister, Yorke, impaling, Qly, 1st and 4th,
Gules a fess chequy argent and azure (Lindsay), 2nd and 3rd, Or a lion
rampant gules debruised by a bendlet sable within a bordure azure
charged with six molets or (Abernethy)   The shields surrounded by
the collar of the Order of the Garter, the George pendent below the
motto
Earl's coronet   Crest: A lion's head erased or collared gules the
collar charged with a bezant   Mantle: Gules and ermine   Motto:
Nec cupias nec metuas   Supporters: Dexter, A lion reguardant or,
the collar gules charged with a bezant   Sinister, A stag proper,
attired or, similarly collared
For Philip, 3rd Earl of Hardwicke, who m. 1782, Elizabeth, dau. of
James, 5th Earl of Balcarres, and d. 18 Nov. 1834. She d. 26 May 1858.
(B.P. 1875 ed.; Cussans)
(There is another hatchment for the 3rd Earl at Whaddon,
Cambridgeshire)

2. Sinister background black
Sable two chevronels or between three herons argent beaked and
legged or (Hearne), impaling, two coats per fess, Gules a fess chequy
argent and azure (Lindsay), Or a lion rampant gules over all a bendlet
sable (Abernethy)
Motto: Resurgam   Two cherubs' heads above shield, which is
suspended from a lover's knot
For Elizabeth Lindsay, who m. Thomas William Hearne, of Deeves
Hall, Ridge, and d. 3 Aug. 1825.   (Cussans; M.I.)

3. All black background
Arms: As 2.
Crest: A cubit arm vested azure cuffed or the hand grasping a roll of
parchment or   Mantling: Gules and argent   Motto: Fortuna et
amicitia
For Thomas William Hearne, of Deeves Hall, Ridge, who d. 19 Feb.
1846, aged 81.   (Source, as 2; M.I.)

4. All black background
On a lozenge   Argent a chevron between three plummets sable
(Jennings), impaling, Sable a chevron between three fleurs-de-lys
argent (Richards)
Motto: Resurgemus
For Jane Richards, who m. William Jennings, and d. 15 Sept. 1809.
He d. 25 Feb. 1809.   (per G. B. Lambert)
(This hatchment was recorded in 1953 in poor condition and has since
been destroyed)   .

5. Sinister background black

Qly, 1st and 4th, Argent a chevron gules between three plummets sable (Jennings), 2nd and 3rd, Sable a chevron between three fleurs-de-lys or (Richards), impaling, Sable ermined argent a trefoil slipped between three round buckles tongues to base argent (Jodrell)
Motto: In coelo quies   Two cherubs' heads above shield
For Louisa, dau. of Richard Paul Jodrell, of Lewknor, Oxon, and Sall, Norfolk, who m. Richard Jennings, of Ridge, and d. 22 July 1826, aged 47. He d. 23 Aug. 1848, aged 67.   (B.P. 1939 ed.; Cussans; M.I.)

6. Dexter background black

Argent a chevron sable ermined or between three bushes on mounds proper (Bushnan)   In pretence: Qly, 1st and 4th, Vert three hillocks argent (Hills), 2nd and 3rd, Sable a lion rampant per fess argent and or (Lloyd)
Crest: A dexter arm embowed vested sable cuffed argent grasping in the hand a roll of paper proper   Mantling: Gules and argent
Motto: In coelo quies   Winged skull in base
For Joseph Bushnan, of Stratford, Essex, who m. Mary Elizabeth, dau. and heir of John Hills of the Isle of Sheppey, by his wife Mary Lloyd, and d. 17 Jan. 1797, aged 52. She d. 16 Jan. 1828, aged 80.
(Cussans; M.I.)

ST ALBANS, Gorhambury

1. Sinister background black

Qly, 1st and 4th, Argent on a fess sable three pierced molets of six points or, in chief an ermine spot, in the 1st quarter the Badge of Ulster (Grimston), 2nd and 3rd, Sable a fess indented between two leopards' faces or (Luckyn)   In pretence: Azure a fess indented between three eagles displayed or (Walter)
Viscountess's coronet   Motto: Mediocria firma   Supporters: Dexter, A stag reguardant proper attired or   Sinister, A griffin reguardant or   Cherub's head above
For Harriot, only dau. and heiress of Edward Walter, of Stalbridge, Dorset, who m. 1774, James Bucknall, 3rd Viscount Grimston, and d. 7 Nov. 1786.   (B.P. 1949 ed.)   (This hatchment is not at present on view to the public; the hatchment of her husband is at Redbourn)

SAWBRIDGEWORTH

1. Dexter background black

Argent a chevron between three millrinds sable (Milles)   In pretence:

Or a chevron gules between three griffins' heads erased sable (Gardiner)
Crest: A hare sejant proper in the mouth three ears of corn or
Mantling: Gules and argent   Motto: Resurgam
For Jeremiah Milles, who m. Rose, dau. and heir of Edward Gardiner
of Pishobury, and d. 22 Apr. 1797, aged 46.   (Cussans)

2. All black background
On a lozenge surmounted by a cherub's head
Arms: As 1.
Motto: Resurgam
For Rose, widow of Jeremiah Milles. She d. 21 May 1835, aged 77.
(Source, as 1.)

3. All black background
On a lozenge surmounted by a cherub's head
Gardiner arms only
Skull below lozenge
Unidentified

4. Sinister background black
Azure ten estoiles, four, three, two and one or (Alston)   In pretence:
Qly, 1st and 4th, Milles, 2nd and 3rd, Argent a chevron between three
griffins' heads erased gules (Gardiner)
Cherubs' heads above shield and gold decoration around
For Rose, dau. and heir of Jeremiah Milles, who m. Rowland Alston, of
Pishobury, 2nd son of Thomas Alston, of Odell, Beds, and d. 16 Feb.
1824, aged 41. He d. 21 Nov. 1865, aged 83.   (Source, as 1.)

5. Dexter background black
Argent three pallets azure over all a bend gules (Annesley), impaling,
Azure a lion rampant or (   )
Crest: A demi-blackamoor proper, wreathed at the temples argent and
azure   Mantling: Gules and argent   Motto: Requiescat in pace
For Alexander Annesley, who d. 15 Dec. 1813, aged 60.
(Cussans; M.I.)

6. Dexter background black
Azure a circular wreath argent and sable with four hawks' bells
conjoined thereto in quadrangle or (Jocelyn), impaling, Gules three
cinquefoils or, on a chief argent a lion passant gules holding in its
dexter forepaw a caltrap azure (Hamilton)
Earl's coronet   Crest: A falcon's leg erased at the thigh proper
belled or   Mantle: Gules and argent   Motto: Faire mon devoir
Supporters: Dexter, A falcon belled or   Sinister, A waterbuck
argent unguled or collared flory gules
For Robert, 1st Earl of Roden, who m. 1752, Anne, dau. and heiress of
James, Earl Clanbrassill, and d. 22 June 1797.   (B.P. 1875 ed.; Cussans)

7. All black background
Qly of six, 1st and 6th, Jocelyn, 2nd, Azure a fess or (Chastellayne),
3rd, Gules a griffin segreant within a bordure engrailed or (Battell),
4th, Gules on a saltire engrailed or five roundels gules a chief ermine
(Hyde), 5th, Azure three cinquefoils or (Bardolf)
Crest: (on a knight's helm) A falcon's leg erased at the thigh,
feathered gules, legs and feet or, claws gules, belled or
Mantling: Gules and argent   Motto: Memento mori
Unidentified

STANSTEAD ABBOTTS, St James (old church)

1. Dexter and top sinister background black
Argent three boars' heads erased and erect sable (Booth), impaling two
coats per fess, in chief, Argent a chevron gules between three roses
gules barbed vert seeded or (Coope), and in base, Ermine a bend gules
(Wallis)
Crest: A lion passant argent   Mantling: Gules and argent
Motto: Deus adjuvat nos
For Philip Booth, of Waltham Abbey, who m. 1st, Elizabeth, dau. of
J. Wallis of London. She d. 10 Nov. 1798. He m. 2nd, Fanny, dau. of
Arthur Coope, and d. 5 May 1818.   (B.P. 1875 ed.)
(Wrongly marshalled; the Coope arms should be in base)

2. Dexter background black
Booth, impaling, Argent on a chevron between three trefoils slipped
azure three crescents or (Williamson)
Crest, mantling and motto: As 1.
For William Booth, of Gunnersbury, Middlesex, and Roydon, Essex,
who m. Mary, dau. and co-heir of John Williamson, of Baldock, Herts,
and d. 17 Oct. 1834, aged 60. She d. 30 Nov. 1848.
(M.I.; B.P. 1875 ed.)
(There is an identical hatchment in the parish church at Roydon, Essex)

3. All black background
On a lozenge suspended from a knot of ribbons
Booth, with crescent for difference   In pretence: Williamson
(trefoils sable)
For Elizabeth, dau. and co-heir of John Williamson, who m. John
Gillyat Booth, brother of William Booth, and d.
He d. Oct. 1849.   (B.P. 1875 ed.)
(There is an identical hatchment in the parish church at Roydon, Essex)

4. All black background
Argent on a chevron azure between three boars' heads erased and erect

sable an estoile of six points argent, in centre chief the Badge of
Ulster (Booth)
Crest: A lion passant argent collared or edged gules holding in the
dexter paw a wreath vert   Mantling: Vert, azure and argent
Motto: As 1.
For Sir Felix Booth, 1st Bt., d. unm. 25 Jan. 1850.
(B.P. 1875 ed.; M.I.)

STANSTEAD ST MARGARET

1. Dexter background black

Qly, 1st and 4th, Argent on a chevron sable, between three roundels
sable the two in chief charged with martlets and that in base with a
trefoil slipped argent, three mascles or (Pratt), 2nd and 3rd, Argent two
bars azure, on a chief azure three leopards' faces argent (Wright),
impaling, Argent three martlets gules, on a chief engrailed gules three
annulets or (Cowper)
Crest: A wolf's head couped at the neck per pale argent and sable,
collared counterchanged, the collar charged with three roundels also
counterchanged
Mantling: Gules and argent   Motto: Resurgam
For the Rev. Joseph Stephen Pratt, Prebendary of Peterborough, and
vicar of St Margaret's, who m. Frances Cecilia, dau. of William Cowper,
and d. 3 Apr. 1838, aged 77. She d. 27 Sept. 1849.
(Cussans, IX; M.I.)

2. All black background

Qly, 1st and 4th, Pratt, 2nd, Cowper (chief not engrailed), 3rd, Wright,
impaling, Qly, 1st and 4th, Azure a chevron between three smelts
naiant argent (Smelt), 2nd and 3rd, Qly ermine and gules (Stanhope)
Crest: As 1, but wolf's head erased   Motto: Resurgam
For the Rev. Charles Pratt, vicar of St Margaret's, who m. Mary Harriet
Smelt, and d. Jan. 1889. She d. 4 May 1855.
(Cussans, X, 140; V.C.H., Vol. 3, 474)

THUNDRIDGE

1. Dexter two-thirds black

Three coats per pale   1. Qly, 1st and 4th, Or a bend engrailed azure
cotised sable (Hanbury), 2nd and 3rd, Vert three acorns erect and
slipped or within a bordure argent (Smith)   2. Or a chevron cotised
between three demi-griffins the two in chief respectant sable (Smith)
3. Qly, 1st and 4th, Argent on a chevron azure three garbs or, on a

canton gules a fret argent (Eardley), 2nd and 3rd, Vert three acorns
erect and slipped or (Smith)
Crest: Out of a mural coronet gules charged with two estoiles of six
points or a demi-lion rampant guardant ermine holding in the dexter
paw a battleaxe argent hafted or   Mantling: Gules and argent
Motto: Industria et providentia
For Robert Culling Hanbury, eldest son of Robert Hanbury, of Poles,
Thundridge, who m. 1st, Caroline, eldest dau. of Abel Smith, of
Woodhall Park, Hertford, and 2nd, Frances Selina, eldest dau. of Sir
Culling Eardley, Bt., of Bedwell Park, Herts, and d. 29 Mar. 1867,
aged 44.   (M.I.s in church and churchyard)

WHEATHAMPSTEAD

1. All black background
On a lozenge   Qly of eight, 1st and 8th, Argent on a fess sable a lion
passant argent (Garrard), 2nd, Azure a wyvern passant wings addorsed
and tail nowed gules (Drake), 3rd, Azure on a bend argent cotised or
a lion passant azure (Tothill), 4th, qly i. & iv. Argent three fusils in fess
gules a bordure sable (Montagu), ii. & iii. Or an eagle displayed vert
armed and membered gules (Monthermer), 5th, Argent three bars
sable a canton sable ermined argent (Marshall), 6th, Gules on a fess
indented argent between six cross crosslets fitchy or three anchors sable
(Raworth), 7th, Argent a chevron engrailed between three escallops
azure (Garneys), impaling, Qly, 1st and 4th, Azure three leopards'
faces argent (Barne), 2nd and 3rd, Argent a chevron azure between
three choughs proper (Asthorpe)
Motto: Resurgam   Cherub's head above lozenge
For Anne, 4th dau. of Miles Barne, of Sotterley Hall, Suffolk, who m.
Charles Drake-Garrard, of Lamer, Herts, and d. 10 Jan. 1827, aged 75.
(B.L.G. 2nd ed.; Cussans, XIV, 338)

HUNTINGDONSHIRE

by

David C. Lane

Kimbolton 4: For Robert, 3rd Duke of Manchester, 1762
(Photograph by Mr. Richard M. Hall)

INTRODUCTION

Huntingdonshire is a small county, though not lacking in historical interest. It contains 39 hatchments, ranging in date from 1720 to 1955, and includes some interesting examples. One particularly fine series, which has recently been restored, is that of the Dukes of Manchester and their alliances; the family seat was at Kimbolton Castle, which is now a school, and the nine family hatchments hang in Kimbolton church. Perhaps because of the nature of the countryside, the remaining hatchments for the most part belong to minor gentry, squires and country clergy. They include an interesting series of seven commemorating members of the Astell family at Everton; these hatchments can only just be claimed for the county, as although the church is in Huntingdonshire the village is in Bedfordshire.

The hatchment of Harriet Rooper at Abbots Ripton is of special interest as it bears a label on the back 'Painted by W. W. Aller in Huntingdon in 1841'. Such labels may not be uncommon, but there is rarely an opportunity to find out, as most hatchments are firmly fixed to the walls. Harriet Rooper's husband, John Bonfoy Rooper died in 1855 in a somewhat unusual manner by falling over the banisters at his house.

Sir Charles Cope, whose hatchment hangs at Orton Longueville, is also commemorated at Hanwell in Oxfordshire, a not uncommon instance of the use of a hatchment at more than one family seat. Woolley church, demolished in 1959, was believed to have contained several hatchments, but their present whereabouts is unknown.

There are no less than three hatchments of the present century; at Holywell for William Ross, d. 1918, and at Diddington for Arthur John Thornhill, d. 1930, and Noel Thornhill, d. 1955.

The Dryden hatchment at Catworth is most unusual, on a wood panel with the arms in low relief. The whole of the hatchment, including the frame, is painted grey. It has, however, been included for it is of the normal diamond shape and is in a frame decorated with foliage, and with a cherub's head at each corner, similar to many hatchments of the late 17th and early 18th centuries.

David C. Lane
100a, Pole Hill Road, Hillingdon, Middlesex

ABBOTS RIPTON

1. Sinister background black
Sable an eagle close or langued gules (Rooper)   In pretence: Azure
on a cross argent a human heart gules (Bonfoy)
Mantling: Gules and argent   Cherub's head above
For Elizabeth, only child of Thomas Bonfoy, of Abbots Ripton, who
m. 1777, John Rooper, of Berkhampstead Castle, and Abbots Ripton,
and d. 14 July 1824.   (B.L.G. 1937 ed.; M.I.)

2. All black background
Arms: As 1.
Crest: On a chapeau gules and ermine a blazing star or   Mantling:
Gules and or (brown)   Motto: Lux anglis crux francis
For John Rooper, who d. 17 Dec. 1826.   (Sources, as 1.)

3. Sinister background black
Qly of six, 1st, Sable an eagle close or (Rooper), 2nd, Or two chevrons
azure (   ), 3rd, Gules a bend between six cross crosslets or (Furneaux),
4th, Sable a pale lozengy argent (Furneaux), 5th, Vairy argent and sable,
on a canton sable a cross patonce argent (   ), 6th, Gules a fess
between two chevrons vair (Goodyer), impaling, Qly, 1st and 4th,
Azure two bars surmounted by a bend or (Pott), 2nd, Gules three
swords palewise in fess argent pommels in base or (Clarke), 3rd, Gules a
cross engrailed between four pheons argent (   )
Cherub's head above
Note on back: Painted by W. W. Aller in Huntingdon in 1841.
For Harriet, only dau. of William Pott, of London, who m. 1813, John
Bonfoy Rooper, and d. 1841.   (B.L.G. 1937 ed.; painter's note)

4. All black background
Arms: As 3.
Crest: As 2.
For John Bonfoy Rooper, who d. 1855.   (Source, as 3.)

CATWORTH

1. All black background
On a lozenge surmounted by a cherub's head
Argent on a chevron azure between three boars' heads erect erased
sable an estoile argent (Booth)
Possibly for Elizabeth, sister of Sir Felix Booth, d. 1846.   (B.P. 1875 ed.)

2. All grey background
A lion salient in chief a sphere between two estoiles (Dryden)
Crest: A demi-lion salient
Mantling, but no motto
An all wood hatchment, c. 2 ft. x 2 ft., in low relief, painted grey
including frame which is decorated with foliage and cherubs' heads
Unidentified

CHESTERTON

1. Dexter background black
Qly, 1st and 4th, Sable on a bend cotised argent three leaves proper
(   ), 2nd and 3rd, Sable on a chevron between three cross crosslets
argent a rose gules (   ), impaling, Gules a fess chequy or and sable
between ten billets four and six argent (Lee)
Crest: A tree proper, to dexter of trunk a fleur-de-lys or   Mantling:
Gules and argent   Motto: In coelo quies
Unidentified

CONINGTON

1. Dexter background black
Qly, 1st and 4th, Ermine three roundels vert each charged with a cross
or (Heathcote), 2nd and 3rd, Argent two chevrons gules each charged
with an ermine spot argent (Moyer), impaling, Barry of six argent and
gules (Thornhill)
Crest: On a mural coronet azure a roundel vert as in the arms between
two wings displayed ermine   Mantling: Gules and argent
Motto: Resurgam
For John Heathcote, of Conington Castle, who m. 1799, Mary Anne,
dau. of George Thornhill, of Diddington, and d. 3 May 1838. She d. 27
July 1854.   (B.L.G. 1937 ed.)

DIDDINGTON

1. Dexter background black
Gules four barrulets and a chief argent, a crescent gules for difference
(Thornhill), impaling, Argent on a saltire sable five fleurs-de-lys or
(Hawkins)
Crest: A maiden's head and shoulders proper, vested or and azure,
ducally crowned or with thorn leaves issuant therefrom proper
No mantling or motto

For George Thornhill, who m. 1780, Mary Anne, dau. of Sir Caesar Hawkins, 1st Bt. of Kelston, Somerset, and d. 22 Sept. 1827. (B.L.G. 1937 ed.)

2. Dexter background black
Gules two bars gemel and a chief argent, on a crescent gules a label argent for difference (Thornhill)   In pretence: Qly, 1st and 4th, Azure three bucks trippant or (Greene), 2nd and 3rd, Or a pallet between two lions rampant sable (Naylor)
Crest: As 1.   No mantling or motto
For George Thornhill, who m. 1809, Charlotte Matilda, dau. and heir of the Rev. Charles Greene, of Hemingford Grey, and d. 19 May 1852. (Source, as 1.)

3. Dexter background black
Qly, 1st and 4th, Gules two bars gemel and a chief argent (Thornhill), 2nd, Greene, 3rd, Or a pale between two lions rampant sable (Naylor), impaling, Gules a fess or ermined sable between three unicorns passant argent (Wilkinson)
Crest: As 1, but vested gules and azure   Mantling: Gules and argent
Motto: Be fast
For George Thornhill, who m. 1845, Elizabeth Mary, dau. of Robert Wilkinson, and d. 4 Feb. 1875.   (Source, as 1.)

4. All black background
Thornhill arms only, as 3.
Crest: As 1, but vested gules and or   Mantling and motto: As 3.
For Arthur John Thornhill, who d. unm. 4 June 1930.   (Source, as 1.)

5. Dexter background black
Thornhill, as 3, impaling, Thornhill
Crest: As 1, but vested gules and or   Mantling and motto: As 3.
For Noel Thornhill, who m. 2nd, Cecily, dau. of the Rev. Arthur Thornhill, and d. 13 Jan. 1955.   (B.L.G. 18th ed.)

EVERTON

1. All black background
Gules a lion passant per pale or and argent between four cross crosslets argent (Astell), impaling, Ermine two bars or over all a lion rampant azure (Bagnall)
Crest: A cross crosslet or entwined with a snake proper   Mantling: Gules and argent   Motto: In coelo quies   Skull below
On frame: William Astell, Died 15 Oct. 1741.
For William Astell, of Everton, who m. 2nd, Mary, dau. of John Bagnall, of Early Court, Berks, and d. 15 Oct. 1741.   (B.L.G. 1937 ed.)

2. Sinister background black

Gules crusilly a lion passant guardant or, on a canton argent an eagle
displayed sable (Astell), impaling, Bagnall
Motto: In coelo quies   Cherub's head above
On frame: Sarah, 1st wife of Richard Astell, died 15 June 1767.
For Sarah, dau. of John Bagnall, of Early Court, Berks, who m. as his
1st wife, her first cousin, Richard Astell, of Everton, and d. 15 June
1767.   (B.L.G. 1937 ed.)

3. Dexter background black

Astell, as 2, impaling, Qly or and gules a label of three points sable
each point charged with three bezants (Kennett)
Crest, mantling and motto: As 1.
On frame: Richard Astell, Esq. Died 23rd Jan. 1777.
For Richard Astell, of Everton, J.P. and D.L., who m. 1st, his cousin,
Sarah, dau. of John Bagnall, of Early Court, Berks, and 2nd, 1770,
Hannah, dau. of the Rev. Benjamin Kennett, Vicar of Bradford, Yorks,
and d.s.p. 23 Jan. 1777.   (B.L.G. 1937 ed.)

4. All black background

On a lozenge surmounted by a cherub's head   Qly, 1st and 4th,
Argent a lion rampant sable langued gules charged on the shoulder with
an escutcheon 'Or a cross formy gules' (Pownall), 2nd and 3rd, Argent
from the sinister a banner fesswise with the arms 'Azure a chevron
between three lions' gambs erased argent in chief an eagle displayed
sable' (   )   In pretence: Qly, 1st, Qly or and gules a label of
three points sable (Kennett), 2nd and 3rd, Azure a chevron ermine in
base an arrow point upwards or, on a chief argent three daws proper,
on a canton gules a molet or (Dawson), 4th, As 1st but no label
On frame: Mrs. Hannah Pownall, widow of Richard Astell Died
5th Jan. 1807.
For Hannah, dau. of the Rev. Benjamin Kennett, Vicar of Bradford,
Yorks, who m. 1770, as his 2nd wife, Richard Astell, of Everton.
He d. 23 Jan. 1777. She m. 2nd, Thomas Pownall, M.P., Governor of
New Jersey, and d. 5 Jan. 1807.   (B.L.G. 1937 ed.; M.I.)

5. All black background

On a lozenge surmounted by a cherub's head   Qly, 1st and 4th,
Astell, as 1,   2nd and 3rd, Argent a chevron sable between three
thorntrees proper (Thornton), impaling, Thornton
Motto: Resurgam
On frame: Elizabeth, widow of William Thornton Astell, Died 9th
Sept. 1809.
For Elizabeth, dau. of Robert Thornton, who m. 1758, her cousin,
William Thornton, who assumed the additional name and arms of Astell,
in compliance with the will of his grandfather, William Astell, and d. 9
Mar. 1809.   (B.L.G. 1937 ed.; note different date on frame)

6. All black background
Qly, 1st and 4th, Astell, as 1, 2nd, Thornton, 3rd, Gules a fess argent
in chief two cubit arms fesswise the hands supporting a chalice or
(Godin), impaling, Or on a chevron gules between three leopards' faces
proper three trefoils slipped or (Harvey)
Crests: 1. A cross crosslet or entwined with a snake proper 2. A
leopard's head proper ducally gorged or   Mantling: Gules and argent
Motto: Sub cruce glorior
On frame: William Astell, Esq., Died 7th Mar. 1847.
For William Astell, of Everton, M.P., who m. 1800, Sarah, only dau. of
John Harvey, and d. 7 May 1847. She d. 15 May 1841.
(B.L.G. 1937 ed.; M.I.; note different date on frame)

7. Dexter background black
Qly, 1st and 4th, Astell, as 1, 2nd, Argent on a chevron gules between
three thorntrees proper three crosses formy fitchy argent (Thornton),
3rd Azure a chalice or (Godin), impaling, Argent three boars' heads
erased close sable langued gules a bordure engrailed gules (Nisbet)
Crests: 1. A cross crosslet or entwined with a snake proper 2. A lion's
head erased sable langued gules gutty argent ducally gorged or
Mantling: Gules and or   Motto: Sub cruce glorior
On frame: John Harvey Astell Esq., Died 17th Jan. 1887.
For John Harvey Astell, of Woodbury Hall, J.P. and D.L., who m.
1853, Anne Emelia, dau. of Robert Parry Nisbet, of Southbroome
House, Wilts, and d. 17 Jan. 1887. She d. 13 Aug. 1907.
(B.L.G. 1937 ed.)

HOLYWELL

1. Dexter background black
Per pale sable and gules two water bougets in chief and a boar's head in
base argent (Ross), impaling, Per chevron engrailed gules and argent in
chief three cinquefoils argent and in base a bear sejant sable muzzled or
(Barker)
Crest: A water bouget argent   Mantling: Sable and argent
Motto: Agnoscar eventu
For William Ross, of Nafferton, Yorks, who m. 1878, Mary Hannah,
dau. of William Barker, of Driffield, Yorks, and d. 2 Aug. 1918, aged 64.
(M.I. in churchyard)

KIMBOLTON

1. Sinister background black
Qly, 1st and 4th, Argent three lozenges conjoined in fess gules a

bordure sable (Montagu), 2nd and 3rd, Or an eagle displayed vert armed
gules (Monthermer)   In pretence: Sable on a cross or five roundels
sable a bordure engrailed or (Greville)   Also impaling Greville
Duchess's coronet   Motto: Disponendo me non mutando me
Supporters: Dexter, A heraldic antelope or, crined, hoofed and tufted
argent   Sinister, A swan, wings elevated argent, langued and ducally
gorged gules
For Dodington, dau. and co-heir of Robert, 4th Baron Brooke, who m.
1690, Charles, 1st Duke of Manchester, and d. 16 Feb. 1720.
(B.P. 1949 ed.)

2. Dexter background black
Qly, 1st and 4th, Montagu, 2nd and 3rd, Monthermer, a crescent for
difference in 1st quarter, impaling, as dexter (no crescent)
Duke's coronet   Crest: A griffin's head couped or beaked sable,
wings expanded sable, gorged with a collar argent charged with three
lozenges gules   Motto: Disponiendo me no mudando me
Supporters: Dexter, as 1.   Sinister, A griffin or beaked and winged
sable   Mantle: Gules and ermine   Arms surrounded with the
Order of the Bath
For William, 2nd Duke of Manchester, K.B., who m. 1723, Isabella,
dau. of John, Duke of Montagu, and d.s.p. 21 Oct. 1739.
(B.P. 1949 ed.)

3. Sinister background black
Qly, 1st and 4th, Montagu, 2nd and 3rd, Monthermer   In pretence:
Sable a chevron or between three castles proper (Dunch)
Duchess's coronet   Motto: As 2.   Supporters: Dexter, as 1.
Sinister, A griffin or forelegs and beak sable, gorged with a collar argent
charged with three lozenges gules   Cherub's head below
For Harriet, dau. and co-heir of Edmund Dunch, of Little Wittenham,
Berks, who m. 1735, Robert, 3rd Duke of Manchester, and d. 25 Feb.
1755.   (B.P. 1949 ed.)

4. All black background
Arms: As 3.
Duke's coronet   Crest: A griffin's head couped, wings expanded or,
gorged with a collar argent charged with three lozenges gules
Motto: Disponiendo no mudando me   Supporters: Dexter, as 1.
Sinister, A griffin or beaked and membered sable gorged with a collar
argent charged with three lozenges gules   Mantle: Gules and ermine
Winged skull below
For Robert, 3rd Duke of Manchester, who d. 10 May 1762.
(B.P. 1949 ed.)

5. Dexter background black
Qly, 1st and 4th, Montagu, 2nd and 3rd, Monthermer, impaling, Argent

on a fess between two bars gemel gules three griffins' heads erased or
(Dashwood)
Duke's coronet   Crest: As 2.   Motto: As 1.   Supporters:
Dexter, as 1.   Sinister, A griffin or, gorged with a collar argent
charged with three lozenges gules   Mantle: Gules and ermine
Winged skull below
For George, 4th Duke of Manchester, who m. 1762, Elizabeth, dau. of
Sir James Dashwood, 2nd Bt., of Kirtlington, and d. 2 Sept. 1788.
(B.P. 1949 ed.)

6. All black background
On a lozenge surmounted by a duchess's coronet   Arms: As 5.
Supporters: As 5.   Mantle: Gules and ermine
For Elizabeth, widow of George, 4th Duke of Manchester. She d. 26
June 1832.   (B.P. 1949 ed.)

7. Dexter background black
Qly, 1st and 4th, Montagu, 2nd and 3rd, Monthermer, a crescent for
difference in 1st quarter   In pretence: Argent three roses and a chief
gules (Sparrow)   Also impaling, Qly, 1st and 4th, Per pale argent
and sable a chevron engrailed counterchanged between three unicorns'
heads erased ermine counterchanged (Dobbs), 2nd, Sable two lions in
in chief counterpassant guardant and one passant guardant in base or
(Dalway), 3rd, Qly ermine and azure a cross or (Osborne)
Duke's coronet   Crest: As 2.   Motto: As 1.   Supporters: As 5.
For George, 6th Duke of Manchester, who m. 1st, 1822, Millicent (d.
21 Nov. 1848), only dau. and heiress of Brig.-Gen. Robert Bernard
Sparrow, and 2nd, 1850, Harriet Sydney, dau. of Conway R. Dobbs,
of Castle Dobbs, co. Antrim, and d. 18 Aug. 1855.   (B.P. 1949 ed.)

8. Dexter background black
Qly, 1st and 4th, Montagu, 2nd and 3rd, Monthermer, a crescent for
difference in 1st and 4th quarters, impaling, Argent a bend of rustres
gules (d'Alten)
Duke's coronet   Crest: As 2.   Motto: As 1.   Supporters:
Dexter, as 1.   Sinister, A griffin or, armed gules, gorged with a collar
argent charged with three lozenges gules
For William, 7th Duke of Manchester, who m. 1852, the Countess
Louise Fredericke Auguste d'Alten, and d. 22 Mar. 1890.
(B.P. 1949 ed.)

9. All black background
On a lozenge surmounted by a cherub's head
Qly, 1st and 4th, Montagu, 2nd and 3rd, Monthermer
Motto: In coelo quies   Skull below
Probably for Lady Dodington Montagu, 2nd dau. of 1st Duke, d. 8
Jan. 1774.   (Note in church)

ORTON LONGUEVILLE

1. Sinister background black
Argent on a chevron azure between three roses gules slipped and leaved proper three fleurs-de-lys or (Cope), impaling, Gules a bend argent between six cross crosslets fitchy or (Howard)
Crest: (defaced) top of a dragon's head gules only visible
Mantling: Gules and argent   Motto: Aequo adeste animo
For Arabella, eldest dau. of Henry, 4th Earl of Carlisle, who m. as his 1st wife, Jonathan Cope, and d. 1746.   (B.E.B.)

2. Dexter background black
Cope, impaling to dexter, Howard, with augmentation, and to sinister, Qly per fess indented or and gules (Leighton)
Crest: Out of a fleur-de-lys or a dragon's head gules   Mantling: Gules and argent   Motto: As 1.
For Jonathan Cope, who m. 1st, Arabella, dau. of Henry, 4th Earl of Carlisle, and 2nd, Jane, dau. of Lieut.-Gen. Francis Leighton, and d. 2 Nov. 1763.   (B.E.B.)

3. Dexter background black
Cope, with Badge of Ulster, impaling, Argent on a bend cotised gules three roundels argent (Bisshopp)
Crest and motto: As 2.   Cherub's head below
For Sir Charles Cope, 2nd Bt., who m. 1767, Catherine, youngest dau. of Sir Cecil Bisshopp, Bt., and d. 14 June 1781.   (B.E.B.)
(There is another hatchment for Sir Charles at Hanwell, Oxfordshire)

4. Sinister background black
Qly, 1st and 4th, Azure a chevron between three boars' heads within a tressure flory counterflory or (Gordon), 2nd and 3rd, Cope, impaling, Qly, 1st and 4th, Argent a shakefork between three molets sable (Conyngham), 2nd and 3rd, Azure a cross engrailed or between four roses argent (Burton)
Countess's coronet   Motto: Stant caetera   Supporters: Dexter, A knight in armour proper   Sinister, A horse argent, mane and tail or, charged with an eagle displayed or
For Elizabeth, dau. of Henry, 1st Marquess Conyngham, who m. 1826, as his 1st wife, Charles, 6th Earl of Aboyne (later 10th Marquess of Huntly), and d. 24 Aug. 1839.   (B.P. 1949 ed.)

5. Dexter background black
Qly, 1st and 4th, Gordon, 2nd and 3rd, Cope, impaling, Sable a chevron or between in chief two bearded men's heads proper and in base a cross moline or (for Pegus)
Marquess's coronet   Crest: A stag's head affronté proper collared argent   Mottoes: (above crest) Bydand   (below shield) Animo

non astutia   Supporters: Two greyhounds argent collared gules
each collar charged with three buckles or
For Charles, 10th Marquess of Huntly, who m. 2nd, 1844, Maria
Antoinetta (d. 10 Aug. 1893), only dau. of Rev. P. W. Pegus, and d.
18 Sept. 1863.   (B.P. 1949 ed.)

6. Dexter background black
Within the Garter, Argent six cross crosslets fitchy, three, two and one
sable, on a chief azure two pierced molets or (Clinton), impaling, Azure
three pelicans vulning themselves argent (Pelham)
Earl's coronet   Crest: Out of a ducal coronet gules five ostrich
feathers argent   Motto: Loyalte n'a honte   Supporters: Two
greyhounds argent collared gules   Mantle: Gules and ermine
For Henry, 7th Earl of Lincoln, K.G., who m. 1717, Lucy (d. 20 July
1736), dau. of Thomas, 1st Lord Pelham, and d. 7 Sept. 1728.
(B.P. 1949 ed.)

GREAT STAUGHTON

1. Dexter background black
Vert on a fess or between in chief two garbs or and in base a sickle
erect argent handle or an arrow proper point to dexter between two
estoiles sable (Duberly), impaling, Qly, 1st and 4th, Chequy argent and
sable (St Barbe), 2nd and 3rd, Gules a bend between six cross crosslets
or (Furneaux)
Crest: A dexter arm embowed the hand proper grasping three ears
of wheat or   Mantling: Gules and argent   Motto: Res non verba
For Sir James Duberly, of Gaynes Hall, who m. 2nd, 1805, Etheldred,
elder dau. of Charles St Barbe, of Lymington, Hants, and d. 26 May
1832.   (B.L.G. 1937 ed.; M.I.)

2. Dexter background black
Duberly, impaling, Gules a lion rampant within a bordure engrailed
argent (Grey)
Crest, mantling and motto: As 1.
For James Duberly, of Gaynes Hall, who m. 1837, Emily Hannah, dau.
of Col. the Hon. William Grey, and d. 3 Mar. 1864.   (B.L.G. 1937 ed.)

GREAT STUKELEY

1. Dexter background black
Qly, 1st and 4th, Sable on a fess argent three leopards' faces gules
(Torkington), 2nd and 3rd, Sable on a fess argent three pierced molets

sable (Stukeley), impaling, Argent a cross engrailed gules between
four water bougets sable (Bourchier)
Crest: A talbot passant argent collared and chained sable
Mantling: Gules and argent
For James Torkington, of Stukeley, who m. 1799, Elizabeth, dau.
of Charles Bourchier, of Hadley Barnet, Herts, and d. 6 June 1828.
(B.L.G. 5th ed.; Alumni Cantabrigienses)

MIDDLESEX

by

J. D. Lee

Harefield 4: For Countess Almeria Brühl, 1794
(Photograph by Mr. D.R. Pratt)

INTRODUCTION

What follows is a record of 80 hatchments existing at least recently in Middlesex and the Middlesex parts of London. They are mostly in Anglican churches; a few rest in houses and other secular buildings. There may well be more to be discovered; Middlesex as a very urban and suburban area has more than its fair share of locked churches. It is too an area lacking in continuous landed gentry secure in their country houses. London still has its aristocracy who may be harbouring hatchments in their town house attics; it is also notable for antique emporia, theatrical suppliers and the like who may give hatchments a home for a while.

It is not possible to put a number to the hatchments which have been lost in Middlesex. A metropolitan county, Middlesex lacks a real published county history, and Lysons' work, the nearest to such, is casual with monuments, never mind hatchments. The present survey is the first attempt[1] to list existing hatchments, aiming, like all the volumes in this series to record these decorative historical records before all are gone, and encourage their preservation. There has been destruction in the 19th and 20th centuries alike. Mills, historian of Hayes, notes that the church had 'a large number' of hatchments before its 19th century restoration; not one remains. The Victoria County History notes West Drayton's 'numerous emblazoned banners' and other funeral impedimenta there in 1849. A disastrous fire at Hackney parish church seems to have carried away that church's tally of six. Rotting canvas picks them off more singly but no less effectively in the long run. The parish churches of Harrow and Chelsea are two others now lacking but once possessed of fine collections.

There are a few good collections left, Ruislip (11) and Harefield (9) the best, with good chronological spread, but Littleton's eight of one family is also worthy of note. Middlesex does not contain any hatchments of historical importance, and no panel/hatchments, though there are monumental panels at East Bedfont and St Margaret's, Westminster, and also modern pseudo-hatchments, two at Greenford and one at Northolt.

The hatchments of few famous people, other than by birth, remain in the area, though it includes most of London. This is perhaps not surprising as (1) most would be found in the churches near their country estates, and (2) although there were many on London town houses ('I walk in Harley Street where every other house has a hatchment', says Thackeray, and they are represented in painting and engravings by Hogarth and many other artists) they would not, by pressure of numbers alone, be kept in churches for long.

Not all the hatchments listed here have been identified, reflecting the lack of a good county history revised in the 19th century. Again the special character of Middlesex as a metropolitan county, close to London (its Guildhall next door to Westminster Abbey), without its county town even, may be mentioned. There were country houses and county families in Middlesex, but one might argue that they were without the self-conscious continuity found in most other counties.

As usual most of the Middlesex and London hatchments are 19th century, the earliest probably about 1705, the latest 1952 (East Finchley). There are only three of the 20th century, though the flurries of correspondence on modern hatchments have shown that it was amongst London Society that the hatchment habit died hard, particularly in Mayfair and Belgravia.

An unusual feature in some London churches should be noted, the presence of royal funeral escutcheons, commemorating royal funerals. Brief details of these are given at the end of the main text, and a discussion of the practice may be found in Mrs. L. B. Ellis' article 'Royal Hatchments in City Churches'.[2]

I should like to take this opportunity to acknowledge with gratitude the help given by members of the Middlesex

Heraldry Society, who have carried out a recent check of all the hatchments, and who have added a further five which were previously unrecorded.

J. D. Lee·
21 Vicarage Way, Rayners Lane, Harrow

NOTES

[1] R. Michael Robbins: *Middlesex parish churches* (London and Middlesex Archaeological Society transactions 18 (2) 1955 noted the presence of many, but without details).

[2] L. B. Ellis: *Royal Hatchments in City Churches* (London and Middlesex Archaeological Society transactions, new series, vol. 10, 1948, 24–40).

BRENTFORD, Syon House

1. All black background
Within the Garter, Qly, 1st and 4th, qly i. & iv. Or a lion rampant
azure (Louvain), ii. & iii. Gules three lucies hauriant argent (Lucy), 2nd
and 3rd, Azure five fusils conjoined in fess or (Percy)
Duke's coronet   Crest: On a chapeau gules and ermine a lion statant
tail extended azure   Motto: Esperance en Dieu   Supporters:
Dexter, A lion rampant azure   Sinister, A lion rampant guardant
ducally crowned or gorged with a collar compony argent and azure
For Hugh, 3rd Duke of Northumberland, K.G., who d.s.p. 11 Feb.
1847.   (B.P. 1963 ed.)
(This hatchment was recorded in 1953 in a private museum in
Twickenham. It appeared later in a London sale-room, was purchased
by the General Editor and returned by him to its original home; there is
another hatchment for the 3rd Duke at Alnwick, Northumberland)

CRANFORD

1. All black background
On a lozenge surmounted by the coronet of a countess
Gules a chevron between ten crosses formy argent (Berkeley), impaling,
Per pale wavy azure and gules a lion passant between three annulets
argent (? for Cole)
Supporters: Two lions argent the sinister ducally crowned, collared,
lined and ringed gules
Probably for Mary Cole, who m. 1796, Frederick Augustus, 5th Earl
of Berkeley, and d. 30 Oct. 1844.   (B.P. 1949 ed.)

EDGWARE

1. Sinister background black
Azure a molet argent within an annulet or (   ), impaling, Argent
on a fess gules between three lions' heads erased sable langued gules
three eagles rising argent (   )
Motto: Resurgam   Two cherubs' heads above shield
Unidentified
(Stolen from the church since the survey began)

133

EDMONTON, All Saints

1. Sinister background black

Or on a fess couped gules between three moorcocks sable a garb or
(Morris), impaling, Qly, 1st and 4th, Gules a rose or (   ), 2nd and
3rd, Argent on a chevron gules between three trees proper three
bezants (   )
Mantling: Gules and argent   Motto: Tramite recto   Cherub's
head above
Unidentified

2. Dexter background black

Azure a chaplet of three oak sprigs joined by an annulet or, on a chief
argent an eagle displayed sable (   ), impaling, Argent three bulls'
heads erased sable (   )
Helm but no crest   Mantling: Gules and argent   Motto: Resurgam
Unidentified

St James, Fore Street

1. All black background

Qly gules and azure a cross flory between four estoiles argent (Snell)
Crest: A wolf preying on a lamb proper in front of a cross formy fitchy
or   Mantling: Gules and argent   Motto: Sublimis per ardua tendo
Unidentified
(Recorded in poor condition in 1966. Church now redundant and
hatchment believed missing)

FINCHLEY

1. All black background

Azure a lion rampant reguardant between three arrows points
downwards or (Gildart)   In pretence: Argent on a mount a savage
man ambulant between two trees, in dexter hand a club resting on his
shoulder, the sinister resting on his hip, all proper (Meyer)
Crest: A sheaf of six arrows three and three points downwards in
saltire or   Mantling: Gules and argent   Motto: Resurgam
For Thomas Gildart, of Moss Hall, Finchley, who m. 1759, Sara, dau.
of Peter Meyer, and d. 30 Oct. 1816.   (per G. B. Lambert)

2. All black background

Qly, 1st and 4th, Per fess azure and gules a chevron rompu between
three griffins' heads erased ermine (Allen), 2nd and 3rd, Sable a

chevron ermine between three unicorns' heads couped argent (Head)
Crest: A griffin's head erased per fess ermine and gules
Mantling: Gules and argent   Motto: Resurgam
Possibly for Thomas Allen, of the Manor House, Finchley, who d.
1 Apr. 1820.   (M.I.)

3. Sinister background black
Argent a chief gules (Worsley)   In pretence: Qly, 1st and 4th,
Gildart, 2nd and 3rd, Meyer
Motto: In coelo quies   Two cherubs' heads above shield
For Elizabeth, dau. of Thomas Gildart, of Moss Hall, who m. 1795,
the Rev. Ralph Worsley, Rector of Finchley, and d. 1831. He d. 1848.
(per G. B. Lambert)

4. All black background
On a lozenge surmounted by a cherub's head
Gules on a bend between six martlets or three roundels gules (Wardle),
impaling, Argent on a fess between three pheons sable a lion passant or
(Atkinson)
Motto: Resurgam
For Ann, dau. of John Atkinson of Finchley, who m. John Wardell,
and d. 30 June 1806.   (C. O. Banks MS, Finchley Central Library,
L 283:42)

EAST FINCHLEY, Holy Trinity

1. All black background
Within the ribbon of the Bath   Argent a spider's web sable, on a
chevron gules four daggers points upwards proper, hilted and
pommelled or, on a chief gules a cross argent having in dexter chief
a lion passant guardant on a crown or (King)   ·
Crest: From a mural coronet or a springbok's head proper ducally
gorged gules   Mantling: Sable and argent   Motto: Duty
Supporters (on a mount proper): Dexter, An antelope proper
Sinister, An eagle sable   Suspended from the shield are the Orders
of the Bath, St Michael and St George, and St John of Jerusalem
A small hatchment, c. 2 ft. x 2 ft.
For Sir Edwin James King, K.C.B., C.M.G., Bailiff Grand Cross of the
Order of St John of Jerusalem, of the Old House, East Finchley, d.
11 July 1952.   (Armorial Families, 1929 ed.)

FRIERN BARNET

1. Dexter background black
Gules a chevron between three boars' heads or (   ), impaling,

Azure three bezants each charged with a martlet sable, a chief or (Pratt)
Crest: A boar statant or   Mantling: Gules and argent
Motto: Grande certamen
Unidentified

2. All black background

On a lozenge surrounded by gilt scrollwork and surmounted by a
cherub's head   Gules a buck's head cabossed or (Down), impaling,
Per pale azure and gules a lion statant reguardant or (Neale)
Motto: Resurgam
For Rose, dau. of Henry Neale, who m. Richard Down, and d. 24 Feb.
1832. He d. 26 July 1811.   (M.I.)

3. Sinister background black

Qly, 1st and 4th, Azure on a chevron argent between three fleurs-de-lys or
three estoiles gules (Sheppard), 2nd and 3rd, Azure a bend ermine
between six molets pierced argent (Hulbert), impaling, Qly of six, 1st
and 6th, Gules a buck's head cabossed argent and or (Down), 2nd,
Neale, with a crescent for difference, 3rd, Per saltire argent and or, in pale
two moorcocks, in fess two escallops sable (More), 4th, Argent on a fess
between three foxes' heads erased sable three molets or (Cleeve), 5th,
Ermine three cats-a-mountain passant guardant in pale azure (Adams)
Two cherubs' heads and olive branches above the shield
For Sarah, dau. of Richard Down, who m. 1800, Thomas Sheppard, of
Folkington Place, Sussex, and d. 24 Apr. 1845.
(B.L.G. 5th ed.; M.I.)

4. Dexter background black

Azure on a chevron argent between two roses argent seeded or and an
anchor or three thistles slipped proper (Pasley), impaling, Argent a
crescent gules, on a chief azure three molets argent (Durham)
Crest: From a naval coronet or an arm in armour embowed proper, in
the hand a staff bearing a flag, Argent a cross gules, on a canton azure a
human leg couped erect proper   Mantling: Gules and argent
Motto: Pro rege et patria pugnans
For Capt. John Pasley, who m. Margaret Durham, and d. 15 Apr. 1858.
(B.P. 1875 ed.; M.I.)

5. All black background

On a lozenge   Arms: As 4.
For Margaret, widow of Capt. John Pasley, d. 19 Feb. 1877. (Sources, as 4)

HACKNEY

The following six hatchments, recorded in 1954, were all destroyed by
fire in 1955.

1. All black background
Argent a lion's head erased sable langued gules between three crescents gules (Newcome), impaling, Sable on a chevron between three picks argent three annulets sable (?Hooke)
Crest: A lion's gamb erased argent   Mantling: Gules and argent
Motto: Resurgam
Probably for the Rev. Peter Newcombe, Vicar of Aldenham, and of Hackney, who m. Anne Hooke, of Basingstoke, and d. 5 Oct. 1738. She d. 1726.   (B.L.G. 5th ed.)

2. All black background
On a lozenge   Sable on a bend argent cotised or three lions' heads erased gules (Boddicoat), impaling, Or on a chevron sable between three French marigolds slipped proper two lions passant respectant or (Tyssen)
For Richard Boddicoat, of Hackney, who m. 1752, Sarah, dau. of Samuel Tyssen, of Hackney, and d. 1759.   (B.L.G. 5th ed.)

3. Sinister background black
Azure on a cross engrailed or, between in dexter chief and sinister base a caltrap and in sinister chief and dexter base a lion rampant argent, five fleurs-de-lys sable (De Kewer), impaling, Chequy argent and sable (St Barbe)
For Elizabeth, dau. of Alexander St Barbe, of Bitterne, who m. John de Kewer, of Hackney, and d.
(B.L.G. 2nd ed.)

4. All black background
Arms: As 3.
Crest: indecipherable   Mantling: Gules and argent
Motto: Resurgam
For John de Kewer, who d.   (B.L.G. 2nd ed.)

5. Dexter background black
Vert a lion rampant guardant argent in chief three molets or (?English), impaling, Sable on a fess or between three elephants' heads erased argent three molets sable (Pratt)
Crest: A lion sejant argent   Mantling: Gules and argent
Motto: Blessed are the dead which die in the Lord
Unidentified

6. All black background
On a lozenge   Arms: As 5.
Motto: Resurgam
Unidentified

HAMMERSMITH, St Paul's

1. All black background
On a lozenge surrounded by gilt scrollwork
Gules on a chevron argent between three leopards' faces or three
crescents gules (Impey)
Probably for Marian, dau. of Sir Elijah Impey, who d. 26 Dec. 1844,
aged 65.   (M.I.)

2. Dexter background black
Qly, 1st and 4th, qly i. & iv. Or an eagle displayed sable (Weston),
ii. & iii. Ermine on a chief sable five bezants (Branthwayt), 2nd and
3rd, Sable on a fess argent between three cross crosslets or three
martlets sable (   ), impaling, Qly, 1st and 4th, Sable three
shacklebolts argent (Anderdon), 2nd and 3rd, Sable an estoile or
between two flaunches ermine (Hubert)
Crest: indecipherable   Mantling: Gules and argent   Motto: In
coelo quies
Probably for Samuel Charles Weston of Rutland Gate, who d. 23 May
1849, aged 57.   (M.I.)
(Unframed, and in poor condition)

3. Dexter background black
Sable three signs of Taurus or, the Badge of Ulster (Bull)
Crest: A bull's head cabossed sable charged on the forehead with the
sign of Taurus or as in the arms   Mantling: Sable and or
Motto: Hitherto
For the Rt. Hon. Sir William James Bull, Bt., P.C., M.P., Maltravers
Herald Extraordinary, who d. 23 Jan. 1931.   (B.P. 1953 ed.)
(There is another, much smaller, hatchment for Sir William at
St Dunstan's-in-the-West, in the City)

HAMPSTEAD, Kenwood House

1. Dexter background black
Two cartouches   Dexter, with Order of the Thistle, Qly, 1st and
4th, Azure three molets argent within a double tressure flory counterflory or (Murray), 2nd and 3rd, Gules three crosses formy or (Barclay)
Sinister, Qly, 1st and 4th, Azure three cross crosslets rising from three
crescents or (Cathcart), 2nd and 3rd, Gules a lion rampant or (Wallace)
Earl's coronet   Crest: A buck's head couped proper, between the
attires a cross formy or   Supporters: Two lions rampant gules
Motto: Uni aequus virtuti   Mantle: Gules and ermine
For David, 2nd Earl of Mansfield, K.T., who m. 2nd, 1776, Louisa, in her
own right Countess of Mansfield, of the 1st creation, dau. of Charles
Schaw, 9th Baron Cathcart, and d. 1 Sept. 1796.   (B.P. 1949 ed.)

HAREFIELD

1. All black background
Gules three lions' gambs erased argent, the Badge of Ulster (Newdigate)
To dexter of main shield, Newdigate, impaling, Ermine two chevronels
azure (Bagot) A.Bl.   To sinister of main shield, Newdigate,
impaling, Gules a chevron between three molets or (Wigginton) D.Bl.
Crest: A fleur-de-lys argent   Mantling: Gules and argent
Motto: Mors janua vitam
For Sir Richard Newdigate, 2nd Bt., who m. 1st, Mary (d. Sept. 1692),
dau. of Sir Edward Bagot, 2nd Bt., and 2nd, 1704, Henrietta, dau. of
Thomas Wigginton, of Ham, Surrey, and d. 4 Jan. 1709-10.
(B.L.G. 1937 ed.; M.I.)

2. All black background
Qly, 1st and 4th, Newdigate, 2nd, Azure three sinister hands couped
argent (Malmains), 3rd, Azure fretty argent (   ), over all a
crescent for difference
Crest and mantling: As 1.   Motto: Mors iter ad vitam
Probably for John Newdigate, 2nd son of Sir Richard Newdigate,
2nd Bt., d. 1705.   (Source, as 1.)

3. Dexter background black
Newdigate, impaling, Qly, 1st and 4th, Azure a cock or (Boucherett),
2nd and 3rd, Sable a fess or between three asses passant argent
(Ayscough)
Crest: As 1..   Mantling: Azure and argent   Motto: Confido
recte agens
For Charles Newdigate Newdegate, who m. 1815, Maria, dau. of
Ayscough Boucherett, of Willington and Stallingborough, Lincs, and
d. 23 Apr. 1833.   (B.L.G. 1937 ed.)

4. Sinister background black
A shield and a lozenge   Dexter, shield, Qly, 1st and 4th, Per pale or
and gules a double-headed eagle displayed per pale sable and argent,
crowned on each head or (Brühl), 2nd and 3rd, Azure a chevron argent
(Brühl), impaling, Paly argent and gules, on a chevron azure three
cross crosslets or (Carpenter)
Count's coronet   Supporters: Dexter, A lion rampant crowned or
Sinister, A horse per fess embattled argent and gules   Sinister,
lozenge, Azure a chevron between three lions' heads erased or
(Wyndham), impaling, Carpenter
Countess's coronet   Motto: Au bon droit   Mantle: Gules and
ermine   Supporters: Dexter, A lion rampant azure winged or
Sinister, as shield   Cherub's head above
For Almeria (Alicia Maria), dau. of George, 3rd Baron Carpenter,
widow of Charles, 2nd Earl of Egremont, who m. 1767, Count John
Maurice Brühl, and d. 1 June 1794.   (D.N.B.)

5. Dexter background black
Sable a stag trippant argent between three pheons or, within a bordure
argent charged with roundels sable (Parker), impaling, Argent three
piles issuant from the chief sable (Anstruther)
Crest: A sheaf of arrows in saltire and pale or, tied with ribbon sable
Mantling: Gules and argent   Motto: In coelo quies   Winged
skull below
For Charles Parker, who m. 1785, Jane, dau. of Sir John Anstruther,
2nd Bt., and d. 24 Apr. 1795.   (B.L.G. 1937 ed.; M.I.)

6. Dexter background black
Sable a fess ermine between three bells argent (Bell), impaling, Argent
on a fess sable three stags' heads cabossed or (? Bradford)
Crest: A swan's head erased or in its mouth a fish proper
Mantling: Gules and argent   Motto: Resurgam   Skull and
crossbones in base
For John Bell, who d. 12 Aug. 1800. His wife, Elizabeth, d. 1829.
(M.I.)

7. All black background
Within Order of the Bath, Paly gules and sable three eagles displayed
argent (Cooke)
Crest: A demi-eagle displayed per pale gules and sable crowned or
Mantling: Gules and argent   Motto: Fortiter in re suaviter in modo
Flags in saltire behind shield
For Sir George Cooke, K.C.B., who d. unm. at Harefield Park, 3 Feb.
1837.   (D.N.B.)

8. Dexter background black
Two shields   Dexter, within the Order of Hanover, Cooke
Sinister, within an ornamental wreath, Cooke, impaling, Azure a
chevron between three lions' heads erased or (Wyndham)
Crest and motto: As 7. Several orders below shield, and flags in saltire
behind it
For Major-General Sir Henry Frederick Cooke, K.C.H., who m. 1834,
Katherine, dau. of Admiral Windham, of Felbrigg, Norfolk, and d.s.p.
10 Mar. 1837.
(B.L.G. 5th ed.)

9. Dexter background black
Qly, 1st and 4th, Or three cross crosslets fitchy gules (   ), 2nd
and 3rd, Gules a lion rampant between three cross crosslets fitchy or
(Capell), over all on a bend azure a dolphin between two roundels
argent (for Spedding), impaling, Qly or and gules on a bend sable five
bezants (? Stebbing)
Crest: From a mural coronet argent a demi-lion rampant proper holding
a garb or and a sword argent hilted or   Mantling: Gules and argent

Motto: In coelo quies
Probably for Robert George Spedding, d. 21 May 1824, aged 66.
(M.I.)

LALEHAM

1. Dexter background black
Qly, 1st and 4th, qly i. & iv. Azure a bend cotised between six crosses
formy or (Bingham), ii. & iii. Ermine a lion rampant gules ducally
crowned or (Turberville), 2nd and 3rd, Per pale gules and argent a
fleur-de-lys per pale argent and sable (Lucan)
Earl's coronet   Crest: On a mound an eagle rising proper
Motto: Spes mea Christus   Supporters: Two wolves proper ducally
gorged and chained or
For Charles, 1st Earl of Lucan, who d. 29 Mar. 1799.   (B.P. 1949 ed.)

LITTLETON

1. All black background
On a lozenge surrounded by gilt scrollwork   Sable a bull passant
argent (Wood)
Motto: In coelo quies   Dated 1666 above the motto
A much later hatchment than the date; probably 19th century
Unidentified

2. Dexter background black
Qly, 1st and 4th, Azure a lion rampant or ducally crowned argent
(Dorrill), 2nd and 3rd, Gules a chevron between three cinquefoils or
(Chambers), impaling, Wood
Crest: From a ducal coronet or a Saracen's head proper wearing a cap
azure fretty or   Mantling: Gules and argent   Motto: Resurgam
For John Chambers Dorrill, who m. Mary Wood, and d.
(B.L.G. 1894 ed.)

3. Dexter background black
Qly or and gules a cross argent (Tuite), impaling, Qly, 1st and 4th,
Wood, 2nd, Argent a stag trippant, between the tines an imperial crown
proper (Williams), 3rd, Argent a chevron between three cocks gules, on
a chief sable three spearheads argent (Williams)
Crest: On a chapeau gules and ermine an angel argent, dexter hand
holding a flaming sword, the sinister resting on a shield of the arms of
Tuite   Mantling: Gules and argent   Motto: Allelujah
For George Gustavus Tuite, who m. Dorothy, dau. of Thomas Wood,
and d. 7 Oct. 1894.   (B.L.G. 1894 ed.; B.P. 1963 ed.)

LITTLETON

4. Dexter background black
Qly, as 3, but chief in 3rd quarter is gules, impaling, Or a bend
countercompony argent and azure between two lions rampant gules
(Stewart)
Crest: A demi-lion rampant or gorged with a wreath azure and gules
between two sprays of oak vert   Mantling: Gules and argent
Motto: Resurgam   Dated 1860 below the motto
For Thomas Wood, M.P., who m. 1801, Caroline, dau. of Robert,
1st Marquess of Londonderry, and d. 26 Jan. 1860.
(B.P. 1963 ed.)

5. All black background
On a lozenge surmounted by a cherub's head, and surrounded by silver
scrollwork
Arms: As 4.
For Caroline, widow of Thomas Wood, d. 10 Aug. 1865.
(B.P. 1863 ed.)

6. Dexter background black
Qly, as 4, with label or on 1st and 4th quarters, impaling, Ermine on a
bend between two unicorns' heads erased azure three lozenges
or (Smyth)
Crest and motto: As 4.   Mantling: Sable and argent
For Thomas Wood, M.P., who m. 1848, Frances, youngest dau. of
John Henry Smyth, M.P., and d. 23 Oct. 1872.
(B.L.G. 1937 ed.)

7. All black background
Qly, 1st, Wood, 2nd, Sable on a bend argent cotised indented or a
molet gules for difference (Clopton), 3rd, Argent a lion rampant
guardant sable debruised by a fess countercompony or and azure
(Mylde), 4th, Gules a saltire between four crosses formy or (   )
Crest: A demi-lion rampant guardant or collared or and azure
Mantling: Gules and argent   Motto: Mors janua vitæ
Unidentified

8. All black background
Wood arms only
To dexter of main shield, Wood, impaling, Argent a chevron sable
between three roses gules (   ) A.Bl.   To sinister of main shield,
Wood, impaling, Per chevron gules and or in chief two ?roses or
(   ) D.Bl.
Crest: As 7.   Mantling: Gules and argent   Motto: Fatum
necessitatis lex
Unidentified

CITY OF LONDON, St Dunstan's-in-the-West

1. Dexter background black
Sable three signs of Taurus or, the Badge of Ulster (Bull)
Crest: A bull's head cabossed gules charged on the forehead with a
sign of Taurus or   Motto: Hitherto
c. 1¾ ft. x 1¾ ft., and fusil shaped; in faded inks on paper and
behind glass
For the Rt. Hon. Sir William James Bull, Bt., P.C., M.P., Maltravers
Herald Extraordinary, who d. 23 Jan. 1931.   (B.P. 1963 ed.)
Despite its unusual construction the hatchment was hung outside Sir
William's house in Cadogan Gardens on his death in 1931.
(There is another hatchment of normal size for Sir William at
St Paul's, Hammersmith)

St James, Garlickhythe

1. Dexter background black
Qly, 1st and 4th, Bendy argent and gules three bucks' heads cabossed or
(Beachcroft), 2nd, Sable a lion rampant or (Mathew), 3rd, Gules a
bend or (Porten), over all a crescent for difference, impaling, Azure a
fess between two lions passant or ermined sable (   )
Crest: A beech tree proper within palings or   Mantling: Gules and
argent   Motto: In coelo quies   Winged skull below
Unidentified

2. Sinister background black
Gules two flaunches ermine, on a chief azure three suns or (Day),
impaling, Gules three lions rampant argent (   )
Motto: In te speravi   Lover's knot and two cherub's heads above
and winged skull below
For Mary, wife of Richard Day, d. 18 Dec. 1788.   (M.I.)

MARYLEBONE, St Mary

1. All black background
On a decorative lozenge   Qly, 1st and 4th, Sable a trefoil slipped
within an orle of molets argent (Phipps), 2nd, Paly argent and azure a
bend gules (Annesley), 3rd, Stuart Britain within a bordure compony
ermine and azure, the latter charged with fleurs-de-lys or (Darnley),
impaling, Qly gules and or, in the first and fourth quarters two
demi-vols in pale or points to dexter, in the second and third an oak
tree eradicated proper charged with an escutcheon gules bearing three
gouttes argent (Thellusson)

For Maria, eldest dau. of Peter Thellusson, of London, who m.
Augustus Phipps, son of Constantine, 1st Baron Mulgrave, and d.
He d. 1826.   (B.P. 1963 ed.)

RUISLIP

1. Sinister background black
Argent a chevron between three bucks courant sable (Rogers), impaling,
Argent a chevron sable between three roundels gules each charged
with an escallop argent (Dacers)
Urn above shield, a cherub's head at each side, and a winged skull
below
For Mary, dau. of Sir Robert Dacers, who m. George Rogers, and d. 8
Feb. 1705.   (M.I.)

2. Sinister background black
Rogers, impaling, Argent four lions passant in bend between two
bendlets sable (Hawtrey)
Motto: Mors janua vitæ
For Jane Hawtrey, who m. James Rogers, and d. 1 Feb. 1735-6.
(M.I.)

3. All black background
Rogers arms only   To dexter of main shield, Rogers, with in
pretence and impaling, Sable six swallows argent (Arundell) A.Bl.   To
sinister of main shield, Rogers, impaling, Argent three lions passant in
bend between two bendlets sable (Hawtrey) A.Bl.
Crest: A buck trippant sable   Mantling: Gules and argent
Motto: Post funera virtus
For James Rogers, who m. 1st Frances Arundell and 2nd, Jane
Hawtrey, and d. 2 July 1738.   (M.I.)

4. All black background
On a lozenge surrounded by elaborate scrollwork
Rogers arms only
Motto: Resurgam
Probably for Elizabeth, dau. of James Rogers, d. 30 Apr. 1803.   (M.I.)

5. Dexter background black
Qly, 1st and 4th, Per pale azure and sable a fess engrailed ermine
between three bulls' heads cabossed or (Emmett), 2nd and 3rd, Azure
two bars argent, on a canton sable a chevron argent charged with a
wolf's head erased sable between two molets gules, between three
pheons argent (Hill)   In pretence: Qly, 1st, Per pale gules and azure
three flies or (   ), 2nd, Argent a lion rampant gules crowned or a

chief azure, on a canton argent an escutcheon azure charged with three
crowns or (St George), 3rd, Argent a cross flory sable (St George),
4th, Gules three covered cups argent (Argentine)
Crest: From a ducal coronet or a demi-bull rampant sable
Mantling: Gules and argent   Motto: Firmitas in caelo
Skull in base
For Henry Emmett, who was bur. at Ruislip, 24 May 1756.
(Bur. register)

6. All black background

Azure six annulets, three, two and one or (Musgrave)
Crest: Two arms in armour embowed argent holding an annulet or
Mantling: Gules and argent   Motto: In coelo quies   Skull in base
Probably for Joseph Musgrave, d. 15 Feb. 1757.   (M.I.)

7. Sinister background black

Gules a lion rampant guardant or, on a chief argent three crescents
gules (Deane), impaling, Gules a chevron between three crescents or
(Gosling)
Motto: In coelo quies
For Elizabeth, dau. of Francis Gosling, of Twickenham Park, who m.
1811, Ralph Deane, of Eastcote House, and of Ruislip, and d. 13
Apr. 1847.   (B.L.G. 1937 ed.; M.I. in churchyard)

8. All black background

Arms: As 7.
Crest: A demi-lion rampant or holding in the dexter paw a crescent
gules   Mantling: Gules and argent   Motto: Virtuti moenia cedant
For Ralph Deane, who d. 10 May 1852.
(B.L.G. 1937 ed.; M.I. in churchyard)

9. Dexter background black

Gules a dexter arm embowed in fess issuant from the sinister or
holding a battleaxe in pale argent (Hingston), impaling, Qly, 1st and
4th, Ermine a millrind sable (?Mills), 2nd and 3rd, Argent a saltire
gules (   )
Crest: A squirrel sejant proper   Mantling: Gules and argent
Motto: Non timide sed caute   Winged skull below
Probably for John Hingston, fl. 1824.   (Encl. Award)

10. All black background

Azure a bend or (Scrope)
Crest: From a ducal coronet or a plume of ostrich feathers azure
Mantling: Gules and argent   Motto: In coelo quies   Cherub's head
at each top angle of shield and skull in base
Probably for Gervase Scrope, d. 1776, aged 68, or Frederick James
Scrope, d. 1780, aged 62.   (B.E.B.)

11. Sinister background black
Gules on a chevron argent three bucks' heads erased sable, a chief per
fess nebuly sable and argent, in chief a crescent for difference
(Woodroffe), impaling, Argent three bucks' heads erased sable collared
or (Hannay)
Motto: Per ardua ad alta   Angel above shield
For Elizabeth (Hannay), who m. George Woodroffe, and d. 2 Sept.
1809.   (M.I.)

GREAT STANMORE

1. All black background
Two cartouches   Dexter, within the Garter, Qly, 1st and 4th,
England, 2nd, Scotland, 3rd, Ireland   In pretence: Hanover
Sinister, Qly of 17, 1st, Azure a lion barry argent and gules (Thuringia),
2nd, Gules an escarbuncle over all an escutcheon argent (Cleves), 3rd,
Or a lion rampant sable (Meissen), 4th, Or a lion rampant to the sinister
sable (Julich), 5th, Argent a lion rampant gules (Berg), 6th, Azure an
eagle displayed or (Saxony), 7th, Or two pallets azure (Landsberg),
8th, Sable an eagle displayed or (Thuringia), 9th, Or semy of hearts
gules a lion rampant to the sinister sable (Orlamunde), 10th,
Argent three bars azure (Eisenberg), 11th, Azure a lion rampant per fess
or and argent (Tonna in Gleichen), 12th, Argent a rose gules barbed
and seeded proper (Burgaviate of Altenberg), 13th, Gules plain
(Sovereign Rights), 14th, Argent three beetles' pincers gules (Engern),
15th, Or a fess chequy gules and argent (Marck), 16th, Per pale, dexter,
Gules a column argent (Roemhild), sinister, Or a cock sable wattled
gules (Hennenberg), 17th, Argent three chevronels gules (Ravensberg)
Over all an escutcheon, Barry or and sable a crown of rue in bend
vert (Saxony)
Imperial crown above   No crest, mantling or motto   Supporters:
Dexter, A lion rampant or   Sinister, A unicorn argent
For Queen Adelaide, dau. of George, Duke of Saxe Meiningen, who
m. H.M. King William IV, and d. 2 Dec. 1849.

2. Dexter background black
Qly, 1st and 4th, Argent a boar's head couped between three crescents
sable (Tennent), 2nd and 3rd, Azure an eagle displayed or (Tovey),
impaling, Or on a chief sable three escallops argent (Graham)
Crests: Dexter, A ship with one sail rising from a mural coronet proper.
Sinister, On a chapeau gules and ermine an eagle displayed or
Motto: Pro utilatate   Three flags, red, white and blue on each side
of shield
For Hamilton Tovey-Tennent, who m. 1836, Helen, only dau. of General
Samuel Graham, and d.s.p. 4 Mar. 1866.   (D.N.B.)

LITTLE STANMORE

1. All black background
Within the Order of the Bath, with badge pendant below, Qly, 1st and
4th, Argent on a cross sable a leopard's face or (Brydges), 2nd and 3rd,
Or a pile gules (Chandos)   In pretence: Azure three pillars or (Major)
Duke's coronet   Crest: The bust of an old man in profile, couped
at the shoulders proper, habited paly argent and gules semy of roundels
counterchanged, wreathed round the temples argent and sable
Mantling: Gules and argent   Motto: Maintien le droit   Supporters:
Two otters argent
For Henry, 2nd Duke of Chandos, who m. 3rd, 1767, Elizabeth, dau. and
co-heir of Sir John Major, Bt., and d. 28 Nov. 1771.   (Complete Peerage)
(Wife's hatchment is at Thornham Magna, Suffolk)

2. Sinister background black
Qly, 1st and 4th, Brydges, 2nd and 3rd, Or a saltire and a chief gules,
on a canton argent a lion rampant azure (Bruce)   In pretence:
Sable three pheons argent (Nicoll)
Marchioness's coronet   Crest: An otter's head argent   Motto and
supporters: As 1.
For Margaret, dau. and heir of John Nicoll, of Southgate, who m. 1753,
as his 1st wife, James, Marquess of Carnarvon (later 3rd Duke of
Chandos), and d. 29 Aug. 1768.   (Complete Peerage)

3. Identical to No. 2.

4. Dexter background black
Qly, 1st, Brydges, 2nd, qly France and England within a bordure argent
(Plantagenet), 3rd, Chandos,.4th, Bruce (canton hidden)   In
pretence: Qly, 1st and 4th, Argent two chevronels between three
human legs couped at the thigh sable (Gamon), 2nd and 3rd, Gules
three conies couchant argent (Coningsby)
Duke's coronet   Crest, motto and supporters: As 1.
Mantle: Gules and ermine   Winged skull in base
For James, 3rd Duke of Chandos, who m. 2nd, 1777, Anne Eliza, dau.
of Richard Gamon, and d. 29 Sept. 1789.   (Complete Peerage)
(Until recently there was another hatchment for the 3rd Duke at
Avington, Hampshire)

5. Identical to No. 4.

6. All black background
On a lozenge surmounted by duchess's coronet
Arms: As 4.   Supporters: Two otters proper
For Anne Eliza, widow of James, 3rd Duke of Chandos, d. 20 Jan.
1813.   (Complete Peerage)

7. All black background
Argent a fess gules between three dragons' heads erased vert (Mutter)
Crest: From a mural coronet gules an arm erect vested or holding in a
glove argent a dragon's head erased vert   Mantling: Gules and argent
Motto: In Christo tutus   Winged skull in base
For the Rev. George Mutter, who d. 14 Aug. 1843.   (M.I.)

8. Dexter background black
Qly, 1st, Azure on a chevron between three lions' heads erased or three
martlets sable (Plumer), 2nd, Argent a fess between two greyhounds
courant sable (   ), 3rd, Argent a bend compony argent gules and
sable cotised gules (Leventhorp), 4th, Gules three towers argent
masoned sable (   ), impaling, Argent ten trefoils slipped, four,
three, two, one azure, a canton gules (Turton)
Crest: A demi-lion rampant argent holding in the dexter paw a palm
sprig vert   Mantling: Gules and argent   Motto: Lucrum est mori
For Sir Thomas Plumer, Master of the Rolls, who m. Marianne Turton,
and d. 24 Mar. 1824.   (D.N.B.)

9. Dexter background black
Lozengy argent and azure, on a chevron or a thistle proper between
two roundels gules (Begg), impaling, a blank (diapered)
Crest: A cross crosslet fitchy gules encircled by two laurel branches
proper   Mantling: Azure and argent
For David Begg, who d. 1868.   (per J. Tindale)

STANWELL

1. Dexter background black
Qly, 1st and 4th, Gules a tower argent within an orle of cross crosslets
and gouttes or alternately (Hambrough), 2nd and 3rd, Sable on a fess
or between two chevronels ermine two fleurs-de-lys vert (Holden),
impaling, Azure on a chevron engrailed argent between three escallops
ermine a cross crosslet fitchy between two annulets azure (Townsend)
Crest: On a mount vert a horse courant argent   Mantling: Gules and
argent   Motto: Honestum utili praefer
For John Hambrough, who m. 1820, Sophia, dau. of Gore Townsend,
of Honington Hall, Warwickshire, and d. 4 Feb. 1863. She d. 16 Feb.
1863.   (B.L.G. 1894 ed.; M.I. in Ventnor, I.O.W.)
(There is an identical hatchment in the parish church at Ventnor, I.O.W.)

WEST TWYFORD

1. Dexter background black
Gules on a bend argent three molets pierced sable, in sinister chief a

bezant (Willan), impaling, Azure two lions combatant or (Carter)
Crest: A demi-lion rampant or holding in the dexter paw a molet pierced
argent   Mantling: Gules and argent   Motto: Resurgam
For Thomas Willan, who m. Christiana Carter, and d. 19 Mar. 1828.
(M.I.)

2. All black background

On a lozenge surmounted by a cherub's head
Gules on a bend cotised between two roundels argent three molets
pierced sable (Willan), impaling, Carter
For Christiana, widow of Thomas Willan, d. 19 May 1837.   (M.I.)

3. Dexter background black

Qly, 1st and 4th, Gules on a bend cotised between two roundels argent
three molets pierced sable (Willan), 2nd and 3rd, Argent a human
heart gules ensigned with a royal crown proper, in chief three molets
pierced azure, within a bordure embattled gules, a crescent for
difference (Douglas)   In pretence: Willan
Crests: Dexter, A demi-lion rampant argent on a mount proper, the
sinister paw resting on a roundel gules, in the dexter paw a sprig
proper   Sinister, A human heart gules ensigned with a royal crown
proper between two wings displayed argent, and on a scroll above the
motto 'Jamais arriere'
Mantling: Gules and argent   Motto: Resurgam
For John Kearsley Douglas-Willan, who m. Isabella Maria, dau. and
heir of Thomas Willan, and d. 6 Aug. 1833.   (M.I.)

4. All black background

On a lozenge surmounted by a cherub's head
Qly, 1st and 4th, Willan, as 3, 2nd and 3rd, Douglas with crown gules
In pretence: Willan
For Isabella Maria, widow of John Kearsley Douglas-Willan, d. 28
Jan. 1862.   (M.I.)

WESTMINSTER, The Abbey

1. All black background

On a lozenge surmounted by a countess's coronet
Qly, 1st and 4th, Vert a lion rampant argent armed and langued gules
(Home), 2nd and 3rd, Argent three popinjays vert beaked and
membered gules (Pepdie of Dunglass), over all an escutcheon or charged
with an orle azure (Landell)
Motto: True to the end   Supporters: Two lions argent armed and
langued gules

For Elizabeth, dau. of William Gibbons, who m. 2nd, William, 8th Earl
of Home, and d. 1784.   (Label on back of hatchment)
(In strong room in library; in very poor condition)

St Margaret's

1. Sinister background black

Qly, 1st and 4th, England, 2nd, Scotland, 3rd, Ireland, impaling, Qly,
1st and 4th, as dexter, with label of three points argent the centre
point charged with a cross gules, 2nd and 3rd, Barry of ten or and sable
a bend treflé vert (Saxony)
For H.R.H. Prince Albert, d. 14 Dec. 1861.
(Frame inscribed: H.R.H. Prince Consort, died 14th Dec. 1861 aetat 43.
Thos Godson & Geo Vacher Churchwardens)

WILLESDEN

1. All black background

Azure on a fess between three lions' heads erased or three choughs
sable (Nicoll)
Crest: A lion's head erased or   Mantling: Gules and argent
Motto: Universa benevolentia
Unidentified

2. Dexter background black

Nicoll, impaling, Argent three roundels gules (   )
Crest and mantling: As 1.   Motto: Resurgam
Unidentified

3. Dexter background black

Sable on a chevron engrailed ermine between three griffins passant or
a lion's head erased sable (Finch), impaling, Or on a bend sable three
dolphins embowed argent (Franklyn)
Crest: A griffin segreant azure semy of bezants and winged or, bearing
an escutcheon or charged with a lion's head erased sable   Mantling:
Gules and argent   Motto: Carpe diem
For Robert Finch, of Dollis Hill, who m. 1820, Mary, dau. of Richard
Franklyn, of Totteridge, Herts, and d. 11 July 1832.
(Burke's Family Records)
(This hatchment was recorded in 1953, in poor condition, and has
since been destroyed)

Royal (and other similar) funeral escutcheons

It seems to have been a London practice to display the funeral escutcheons of members of the royal family during the period of mourning. Such escutcheons were certainly produced for provincial funerals, but are not known to have been preserved; in the City of London some certainly are. The practice is discussed in detail in Mrs. L. B. Ellis' article (note 2). To those dealt with there may be added the three at St Magnus. In the following list the escutcheons are lozenge shaped, painted on silk, and framed and glazed, unless stated otherwise. All are very much smaller than normal hatchments.

St Mary at Hill

1. All black background   Rectangular
Arms on a cartouche and a lozenge, set on a mantle gules and ermine, with royal crown above
Cartouche, within the Garter, Arms of William IV   Lozenge, Arms of William IV, impaling, Qly of twenty, Brunswick, etc.
Supporters: Dexter, A lion rampant guardant crowned or   Sinister, A unicorn argent, armed, crined and gorged with a coronet or
For Queen Adelaide, widow of William IV. She was dau. of George Frederick, Duke of Saxe-Meiningen, and d. 2 Dec. 1849.
(B.P. 1963 ed.; Ellis illus. 1)

2. All black background
Royal arms as used by George IV and William IV, within Garter, surmounted by royal crown   Supporters: Lion and unicorn
For George IV and William IV. The former d. 26 June 1830, the latter 20 June 1837. The escutcheon was actually used for both periods of mourning.   (B.P. 1963 ed.; Ellis illus. 3)

3. Sinister background black   Rectangular
Two oval cartouches, each within a Garter   Dexter, Royal arms as used by Victoria, with royal crown   Sinister, Qly, 1st and 4th, Royal arms modern, a label of three points argent, charged on centre point with a cross gules, 2nd and 3rd, Barry of ten or and sable, a crown of rue in bend vert (Saxony) Crowned with a foreign royal crown
For Prince Albert, Prince Consort of Victoria, d. 14 Dec. 1861.
(B.P. 1963 ed.; Ellis illus. 4)

St Mary-at-Hill

4. Dexter background black
Two shields   Dexter, with Garter, Royal arms as used by William IV,

but without the crown above the inescutcheon, and without the crown
of Charlemagne, and with a label of three points argent, the centre
point charged with a cross gules, the others with a fleur-de-lys azure
Sinister, Qly of twenty-three, Thuringia, etc.
For Victoria, Duchess of Kent, dau. of Francis, Duke of Saxe-Coburg-
Saalfeld, mother of Queen Victoria, and widow of Edward Augustus,
Duke of Kent and Strathearn. She d. 23 Mar. 1861.
(B.P. 1963 ed.; Ellis illus. 2)
(This escutcheon has been missing for some years)

St James Garlickhythe

1. Sinister background black   Rectangular
Two ovals, on mantle gules and ermine, surmounted by two different
royal crowns   Dexter, Qly of eighteen, Thuringia, etc.   Sinister,
Qly of eighteen, as dexter, impaling, Royal arms as used by George IV,
without crown over the inescutcheons, and without the crown of
Charlemagne
Supporters: Lion and unicorn   Motto: La mort est inevitable
For Princess Charlotte Augusta, wife of Prince Leopold George
Frederick of Saxe-Coburg, and dau. of George IV. She d. 6 Nov. 1817.
(B.P. 1963 ed.; Ellis illus. 7)

2. All black background   Rectangular
Two ovals on a mantle gules and ermine, with royal crown above, which
is surmounted by a royal crest   Dexter, within the Garter, Royal
arms, as used by George III   Sinister, Qly of six, Mecklenburg etc.,
with inescutcheon of Schwerin
Supporters: Lion and unicorn   Motto: Dieu et mon droit
For George III, who d. 29 Jan. 1820.   (B.P. 1963 ed.; Ellis illus. 5)

The two following escutcheons have been lost for some years

3. All black background
Within the Garter, Royal arms, with crowned Hanoverian escutcheon
Supporters: Lion and unicorn
For George III, George IV or William IV.   (B.P. 1963 ed.; Ellis illus. 3)

4. Dexter background black   Rectangular
Two ovals on mantle gules and ermine, crowned, with a crest above the
crown Dexter, within the Garter, Royal arms, with inescutcheon of
Hanover, crowned   Sinister, Qly of eighteen, Thuringia, etc.
Supporters: Lion and unicorn   Motto: Dieu et mon droit
Mantling: Ermine and or, with helm above sinister shield
For William IV, who d. 20 June 1837.   (B.P. 1963 ed.; Ellis illus. 6)

St Edmund King and Martyr

The following escutcheons were formerly at the church of All Hallows, Lombard Street

1. Sinister background black   Rectangular
Two ovals, the dexter within the Garter
Details as for St James Garlickhythe 1.
For Princess Charlotte Augusta, who d. 6 Nov. 1817.
(B.P. 1963 ed.; Ellis illus. 8)

2. Dexter background black
Two oval shields, surmounted by royal crown of prince   Dexter, within the Garter, Royal arms Hanoverian, but without crown and without crown of Charlemagne, and with a label of three points argent, the centre charged with a cross gules, the others charged each with a fleur-de-lys azure   Sinister, Qly of eighteen, Thuringia etc. Supporters: Lion and unicorn, each charged with a label as in the arms
For Edward Augustus, Duke of Kent and Strathearn, son of George III, d. 23 Jan. 1820.   (B.P. 1963 ed.; Ellis illus. 9)

3. All black background
Royal arms Hanoverian, with crowned inescutcheon
Details as St Mary at Hill, 2.
For George III, who d. 29 Jan. 1820, or George IV, who d. 26 June 1830.   (B.P. 1963 ed.; Ellis; Gerald Cobb)

St Magnus the Martyr

1. Sinister background black   Rectangular
Two cartouches, with large royal crown above
Dexter, within the Garter, Royal arms as used by George III   Sinister, Qly of six, Mecklenburg, etc., with inescutcheon of Stargard
For Queen Charlotte, wife of George III and dau. of Charles, Duke of Mecklenburg-Strelitz. She d. 17 Nov. 1818.   (B.P. 1963 ed.)

2. Sinister background black   Rectangular
Arms on two ovals, the dexter within the Garter
Details as for St James Garlickhythe 1.
For Princess Charlotte Augusta, who d. 6 Nov. 1817.
(B.P. 1963 ed.; Ellis illus. 3)

3. Sinister background black   Rectangular
Arms on two cartouches, with large crown above
Dexter, within the Garter, Royal arms as used by George IV, with

crowned inescutcheon   Sinister, within a wreath, Qly of twelve,
Luneberg, etc.
For Queen Caroline, dau. of Charles, Duke of Brunswick-Wolfenbuttel,
and wife of George IV. She d. 7 Aug. 1821.   (B.P. 1963 ed.)
(These three escutcheons are in poor condition although framed)

Christ Church, Greyfriars

According to Mrs. Ellis, and to Arthur J. Jewers (Guildhall MS 2480)
this church contained three further funeral escutcheons, to the Dukes
of Kent, Sussex and Cumberland.

Museum of London

1. Dexter background black   Rectangular

Arms on shield, surmounted by a crown   Qly, 1st and 4th, Argent
a cross gules (St George, for England), 2nd, Azure a saltire or (St
Andrew, for Scotland), 3rd, Azure a harp or, stringed argent (Ireland),
over all an inescutcheon, Sable a lion rampant argent (Cromwell),
impaling, Sable three panthers passant in pale or semy of roundels
sable (Bourchier)
For Oliver Cromwell, Lord Protector, who m. Elizabeth, dau. of Sir
James Bourchier, of Tower Hill, and d. 3 Sept. 1658.   (D.N.B.)
(The escutcheon was used at the Protector's funeral, 23 Nov. 1658)

SELECT BIBLIOGRAPHY

P. G. Summers, *How to read a Coat of Arms* (National Council of Social Service, 1967), 17-20.

P. G. Summers, *The Genealogists' Magazine*, vol. 12, No. 13 (1958), 443-446.

T. D. S. Bayley and F. W. Steer, 'Painted Heraldic Panels', in *Antiquaries Journal*, vol. 35 (1955), 68-87.

L. B. Ellis, 'Royal Hatchments in City Churches', in *London and Middlesex Arch. Soc. Transactions* (New Series, vol. 10, 1948), 24-30 (contains extracts from a herald-painter's work-book relating to hatchments and 18th-century funerals).

C. A. Markham, 'Hatchments', in *Northampton & Oakham Architectural Soc. Proceedings*, vol. 20, Pt. 2 (1912), 673-687.

INDEX